Developing Practical Responses to Social Media Threats Against K–12 Schools

An Overview of Trends, Challenges, and Current Approaches

PAULINE MOORE, BRIAN A. JACKSON, JENNIFER T. LESCHITZ, NAZIA WOLTERS, THOMAS EDWARD GOODE, MELISSA KAY DILIBERTI, PHOEBE FELICIA PHAM

HS AC

HOMELAND SECURITY
OPERATIONAL ANALYSIS CENTER

About This Report

The U.S. Department of Homeland Security's (DHS's) Cybersecurity and Infrastructure Security Agency (CISA) asked the Homeland Security Operational Analysis Center (HSOAC) to provide enhanced tools for kindergarten through 12th grade (K–12) schools and school systems to improve school safety. As part of this task, HSOAC analysts drafted a series of reports based on comprehensive literature reviews of school safety and security and interviews with stakeholders from the K–12 school community. This report draws on the existing literature and guidance for schools on assessing social media and/or anonymous threats against schools. We also draw on data collected on social media threats against schools, as well as information from a series of interviews with federal-, state-, district-, and local-level stakeholders from across the country to discuss their practices to assess and respond to social media threats against schools. The primary audiences for this research are school- and district-level administrators and school safety personnel. State, local, tribal, and territorial government and law enforcement personnel, as well as school-related associations and stakeholder groups, might also be interested in this research. A note to readers: This report contains material about school violence that some may find distressing.

This research was sponsored by CISA's Infrastructure Security Division's School Safety Task Force and conducted within the Infrastructure, Immigration, and Security Operations Program of the RAND Homeland Security Research Division (HSRD), which operates the Homeland Security Operational Analysis Center (HSOAC).

About the Homeland Security Operational Analysis Center

The Homeland Security Act of 2002 (Section 305 of Public Law 107-296, as codified at 6 U.S.C. § 185) authorizes the Secretary of Homeland Security, acting through the Under Secretary for Science and Technology, to establish one or more federally funded research and development centers (FFRDCs) to provide independent analysis of homeland security issues. The RAND Corporation operates the Homeland Security Operational Analysis Center (HSOAC) as an FFRDC for the U.S. Department of Homeland Security (DHS) under contract 70RSAT22D00000001.

The HSOAC FFRDC provides the government with independent and objective analyses and advice in core areas important to the support of policy development, decisionmaking, alternative approaches, and new ideas on issues of significance. HSOAC also works with and supports other federal, state, local, tribal, and public- and private-sector organizations that make up the homeland security enterprise. HSOAC's research is undertaken by mutual consent with DHS and is organized as a set of discrete tasks. This report presents the results of research and analysis conducted under task order 70RCSJ22FR0000005, K–12 Social Media

Response. The results presented in this report do not necessarily reflect official DHS opinion or policy.

For more information on HSRD, see www.rand.org/hsrd. For more information on this publication, see www.rand.org/t/RRA1077-5.

Acknowledgments

We are grateful for the candid and insightful contributions of numerous stakeholders across the K–12 school and law enforcement communities who participated in interviews about social media and other threats that have affected their communities. Their willingness to share their experiences and provide input was invaluable to our work and to helping K–12 communities nationwide navigate similar challenges. We thank our sponsors at CISA, whose support and feedback helped create a research product that we hope will benefit local education agencies, law enforcement personnel, and other relevant stakeholders. We gratefully acknowledge David Riedman for his assistance in utilizing his K–12 School Shooting Database (SSD; 2023) for the project. As part of the review process for this document and the preparation of related documents, we engaged a panel of experts to provide input into our work. We acknowledge the wealth of invaluable expertise they brought to the table and their contributions to improving our research. Finally, we would also like to thank our reviewers, Bob Harrison and Heather Schwartz, for their valuable feedback.

Summary

In a fall 2022 survey of kindergarten through 12th grade (K–12) teachers across the United States, about one-third (35 percent) reported that their school had been disrupted by social media threats from students during the 2021–2022 school year (Jackson et al., 2023). More than half of those teachers reported that this had happened more than once during the same school year. Indeed, news reports from mid-2023 point to the "overwhelming numbers of threats" made to schools in the 2022–2023 school year, some from students and but most made anonymously (Ward, 2023). The Federal Bureau of Investigation (FBI) reported that 6,000 threats were made against schools in 2022, a 60 percent increase nationwide from the previous year; most were posted on social media (Haskell, 2023).

By now, shooting events and threats of shootings shape the educational environment for many schools across the country. As of this writing, it is not uncommon for schools and school districts across the country to receive threats of violence, many issued on various social media platforms commonly used by students and youth more generally, and many of them anonymous. Indeed, the internet and social media give the impression of total anonymity, which can make individuals more comfortable saying or doing things online that they would otherwise not do in person. With this comfort has come a rise in anonymous threats to schools and other public spaces via social media (Ward, 2023).

School threats are defined as "written or verbal threats to attack students" (Haskell, 2023); they can also target other members of the school community, including teachers and other school staff. The scope of this study focuses on social media–based threats specifically, and the range can be broad: An unknown user states on social media that there is a bomb at a specific school; another claims that they are bringing a gun to school the next day to shoot someone specific or anyone at the school more generally. Other threats posted to social media might just be images of someone with a gun, telling others to "not come to school" on a specified date, or vague statements about a mass school shooting that do not mention a specific school location (Ward, 2023).

The overwhelming majority of these threats are either meant to be jokes or to create havoc across a school or district, but they can sometimes be cries for help. Their timing can be random or follow a disturbing pattern: Often, the occurrence of actual, highly publicized mass shootings prompts an onslaught of so-called copycat threats of subsequent shootings, most of them eventually deemed unfounded but leaving schools no choice but to treat each one as a potentially viable threat (Santucci, 2022). At other times, they are responses to trends on social media, such as the "National Shoot Up Your School" trend that plagued schools across the United States in December 2021 (Mak, 2021). The resources that schools must devote to investigating and tracking down the source of each threat, even though most turn out to be hoaxes, are significant. Local law enforcement partners are also forced to respond and expend significant resources in the process. The resulting lockouts, lockdowns, and school cancelations that schools are often forced to implement have a severe emotional toll on students, teachers, and school staff across the country.

What can K–12 schools do to mitigate the impact of these threats, and how can they work with local and other partners to do so? This report sheds light on trends in anonymous threats of violence against K–12 schools posted to social media. It highlights the impact that these threats are having on school communities and the approaches that K–12 schools and their local partners are taking to assess their credibility and decide on the best response. The report is part of a larger effort by the Cybersecurity and Infrastructure Security Agency's (CISA's) School Safety Task Force to provide enhanced tools for K–12 schools and their partners to improve school safety through the development of a related and forthcoming government-published toolkit on social media–based threats as well as additional tools, including *Improving School Safety Through Bystander Reporting: A Toolkit for Strengthening K-12 Reporting Programs* (CISA and NTAC, 2023); the *K–12 School Security Guide* (CISA, 2022); the "School Security Assessment Tool (SSAT)" (CISA, undated); and associated K–12 school physical security training companions.

This research drew on a review of literature focused on assessing and responding to anonymous threats within and outside the K–12 school environment, with particular attention to identifying strategies and practices to assess the viability of such threats, as well as strategies to inform response. The research team also conducted over 40 interviews with stakeholders across the K–12 school community in the United States and local-, state-, and federal-level law enforcement agencies to understand trends in social media–based threats, what schools and their partners are doing to address them, and the challenges that they face doing so. We also draw on analyses of news reports about social media threats made against schools nationwide between 2012 and 2022.

The audience for this report includes a variety of stakeholders. In addition to providing guidance on social media–based threats issued by CISA, we also intend to make this report accessible to local education agencies, individual schools, and law enforcement agencies across the country.

Our research has five main implications for addressing social media threats of violence against K–12 schools:

- **Investigating social media threats—particularly anonymous ones—needs to be a multidisciplinary effort.** School administrators are not usually trained investigators and should be able to rely on local law enforcement partners and other specialists to assess the credibility of threats. School resource officers (SROs) in particular can be a key liaison between the two entities in this area. Sharing responsibilities allows for local education agencies and law enforcement personnel to draw on one another's unique capabilities during the threat investigation process and has been critical to making difficult and potentially high-stakes decisions in response to threats. Stakeholders involved in multiagency responses should establish clear command and control protocols early in the process to ensure that both the investigation and response processes are effective and efficient.

- **Local education agency approaches to navigating social media threats need to balance risks of both under- and over-responding and integrate options for escalation as new information about a threat comes in.** When responding to a threat, schools must balance the risk that a threat might be credible with the trauma and disruption that repeated responses to hoax threats induce. One way to strike this balance is through less overt response strategies that start at lower intensity but can be scaled up rapidly. Integrating certain lower intensity actions when responding to more commonplace and nonviolent emergencies—such as locking school buildings' exterior doors and temporarily adding a uniformed law enforcement officer to school grounds—can also habituate students and staff to certain response measures and potentially alleviate the fear and trauma they might otherwise cause. Finally, establishing a strong reporting culture in which students, parents, and others immediately report threats when they become aware of them can also give decisionmakers more time to make critical response decisions.

- **Local education agencies nationwide would benefit from an established "standard of care" for addressing social media–based and other anonymous threats of violence.** The potential for litigation resulting from both under- and over-response to threats emphasizes the need to develop a "standard of care" around threat response, either at the federal, state, or local level. Responses currently are quite varied. Standards should provide guidance to local school decisionmakers for (1) how to assess the viability of threats; (2) the pathways for balancing response and escalating responses to threats based on new information; (3) common vocabulary used to describe response options implemented by both schools and law enforcement (e.g., "secure hold"); and (4) how to communicate with families and the broader community during a threat response. Specific approaches will need to be customized to meet the needs of individual school districts, and practices developed by leading districts could be vetted by multidisciplinary panels of experts.

- **Local education agencies and their law enforcement partners need new approaches for deterring and detecting social media and other hoax threats.** Because of the significant impact that even hoax threats can have on K–12 school communities, there is a need to prioritize strategies to deter individuals from making them. While there is broad agreement about imposing severe consequences on individuals threatening U.S. schools from abroad, the story is more complicated when it comes to determining consequences for students making threats against their own school. Our research suggests that deterrence strategies could adhere to principles guiding existing threat assessment efforts, which prioritize changing behavior without imposing potentially lifelong consequences for poor decisions made as a youth. Given these challenges, efforts may be best placed on providing students, parents, and others with information regarding the potential consequences—including legal consequences—of making threats against schools, even if these are intended as jokes, at the beginning of each school year.

    If schools choose to use tools to detect threats in student writing (including on social media), these tools need to be improved to be more accurate, limit bias, and limit privacy and civil liberties concerns. When schools do select to use these services, administrators should make clear to their communities what service they are using, what the service monitors for and the purpose behind its use, and they should be vigilant in considering any ways that such tools could introduce biases in how threats are flagged that disproportionately affect different student populations (Schwartz et al., 2022).

- **Future research should focus on improving the options available to local education agencies and public safety agencies dealing with online threats.** Though the insights from our interviewees detail how schools are currently dealing with social media threats, our work also emphasizes the need for continued efforts to improve on today's promising practices. Collecting data on which responses minimize the disruptive and traumatic effect of anonymous threats could ease decisionmaking burdens for school officials. Additional studies of which indicators have the greatest value in distinguishing real from hoax threats (and how those indicators shift as threateners change their behavior) could also help schools and police better navigate the issue, as could leveraging data from school districts that use monitoring software to identify threatening language. Efforts can also focus on better integrating principles for assessing anonymous threats specifically into commonly employed threat assessment guidelines, such as those developed by the U.S. Secret Service's (USSS's) National Threat Assessment Center (NTAC). Continued attention to these and other issues is critical to understanding how the threat landscape is changing, how individuals are turning to new technologies to threaten K–12 schools, and what schools can do to better assess and respond to threats.

Contents

Figures and Tables

Figures

Tables

CHAPTER 1

Introduction

In early 2023, the Federal Bureau of Investigation (FBI) reported that it had received nearly 6,000 reports about school threats in 2022, a 60-percent increase from the previous year (FBI, 2023). Since then, kindergarten through 12th grade (K–12) schools have continued to face the challenge of addressing various threats of violence, most posted to social media or other online mediums and many of them anonymous (Ward, 2023). Indeed, the internet and social media give digital spaces an aura of anonymity, increasing the extent to which individuals feel comfortable doing and saying things online that they might not otherwise do in person. The anonymous threats that schools receive run the gamut. Some are Instagram posts advertising a "school riot" the following day, while others warn of a planned mass shooting. Some have been bomb threats, and others have targeted specific individuals or groups with violence. Some threats are so general as to not name a specific school or district, containing simply a picture of a weapon or even a picture of a picture (often of a fake weapon). School and district officials have reported threats coming from "fake accounts [or] dummy accounts," identified after a lengthy investigation process (Natanson and Meckler, 2021).

These social media threats often spread in the aftermath of actual school shootings, such as the one that took place at Oxford High School in Oxford, Michigan, in November 2021. After that tragedy, at least 60 schools closed across the state when they received shooting threats throughout the month of December 2021 (Natanson and Meckler, 2021). But the trend was not limited to Michigan; according to experts, schools across the country received more than 150 threats of shootings in just the single week after Oxford (Natanson and Meckler, 2021). In the month that followed the mass shooting at Marjory Stoneman Douglas High School in Parkland, Florida, that killed 17 students and teachers in February 2018, there were as many as 70 threats being made against schools every day (Lombardo, 2018).

It turns out that most of these threats are baseless. In December 2021, for instance, no real threats against schools were ever identified. Most of the copycat shooting threats that inundated schools after the Marjory Stoneman Douglas High School attack were also eventually determined to be non-credible. Nevertheless, each threat a school or district receives forces them and their local law enforcement partners into high alert, not knowing whether it is real or not. Every threat, in other words, must be treated as real before it can be deemed a hoax.

The implications for schools and their local partners are significant. In the case of social media–based threats in particular, the investigation process is complicated by the fact that threats often come from fake accounts (Natanson and Meckler, 2021). Images that circulate on social media—for example, a photo of an adolescent holding a gun—may or may not be real. These photos, along with threatening language such as "Don't come to school tomorrow" on a specific school's social media page or an associated page, such as a parent-teacher association's Instagram and Facebook page, prompt fear of an attack. School staff and local law enforcement partners must scramble to determine the origin of the post and the identity of the individual linked to the originating account, a time-consuming process that frequently occurs after school hours, on weekends, or during holiday breaks. When posts like these are continuously shared and reposted by hundreds of users, the process of identifying the original post to assess the threat's ultimate viability becomes especially complex and time-consuming. Frequently, the threatening photo or text post turns out to be from another community altogether (Natanson and Meckler, 2021).

Not only are schools forced to take on the task of assessing each threat they receive, but they must also make difficult decisions around how best to respond: Should the school go into one of various lockdown options, and if so, which one? Is it best to close school altogether or follow some other procedure? Any of these options—whether it involves a move to virtual learning, locking exterior doors and restricting movement into and out of schools, or fully restricting movement inside the school (a full lockdown)—disrupts learning and has other impacts on the school community. The COVID-19 pandemic, for example, significantly increased anxiety and stress among the K–12 student population across the country (Middleton, 2020); returns to virtual learning because of threats, even if short-lived, have the potential to retraumatize many students. Moreover, the recent finding that active shooter drills in K–12 schools—many of which involve practicing lockdowns—increase anxiety, stress, and depression among students suggests that a rise in lockdowns associated with soaring levels of social media–based and other threats against schools is also likely to have a detrimental impact on student well-being (FBI, 2023; Ward, 2023; Yousef, 2022; ElSherief et al., 2021). Threats also increase fear and anxiety among teachers, other school staff, and parents. How best to communicate to the broader community is another serious challenge that schools face when they receive threats, insofar as they must often balance the need to provide enough consistent information to reassure the community while not impeding active law enforcement investigations.

As of this writing, there is relatively little guidance for local education agencies to draw on to design their response to anonymous social media–based threats. School districts across the country have been forced to develop their own approaches to investigate threats and make decisions for how to respond, often placing the weight of the decision on school administrators. Many local education agencies have drawn on the expertise of diverse local partners, such as law enforcement agencies and mental health providers, albeit to various extents and in different ways, depending on their unique contexts. Responses to some older types of threats, such as bomb threats, provide some templates but do not fully address the complications of these new types of threats. Overall, it is unclear what works best and which entities can provide the most support to local education agencies as they continue to grapple with what is likely to be a persistent issue.

Purpose and Approach

This report seeks to shed additional light on how K–12 schools across the United States are being targeted by social media threats, as well as what they are doing to investigate each threat's credibility, ensure the safety of their communities, and work with local and other partners in these areas. The report contributes to ongoing efforts by the Cybersecurity and Infrastructure Security Agency's (CISA's) School Safety Task Force to provide enhanced tools for K–12 schools and school districts to improve school safety through the development of the *K–12 School Security Guide* (CISA, 2022), "School Security Assessment Tool (SSAT)" (CISA, undated), *Improving School Safety Through Bystander Reporting: A Toolkit for Strengthening K–12 Reporting Programs* (CISA and NTAC, 2023), and various K–12 school physical security training companions. This set of tools is designed to help local education agencies build safe and secure learning environments that contribute to the achievement of schools' educational missions.

The study is based on a mixed-methods approach:

- First, we conducted a literature review of over 65 sources focused on means for assessing and responding to threats made against schools via social media. This review included a focused search of state-level sites related to school safety (e.g., safety centers, departments of education) to identify any existing guidance on such threats or guidance about related threats such as swatting incidents (that is, prank calls made to emergency dispatch centers about an ongoing active shooter attack meant to prompt a significant law enforcement response). Because the school-specific literature that specifically addresses this issue is still limited, we also drew on over 50 analyses in comparable contexts that hold appropriate and translatable lessons for the K–12 school environment, such as the literature on assessing anonymous threats from fixated individuals, threats to public officials, and bomb threats.
- Second, and in conjunction with the literature review, we collected and reviewed over 1,000 news reports about incidents of social media threats of violence against K–12 schools across the country. The purpose of this step was to help identify any discernable trends in social media–based threats to schools, including information about their timing, geographical scope, type of school targeted, and, to the extent possible, how schools across the United States were responding to these threats for the time period under analysis (August 2012–September 2022).
- Finally, we conducted 40 interviews with 62 federal, state, school district, and local community stakeholders involved in responding to threats against schools in order to improve our understanding of trends, how social media threats are investigated, how

schools and their partners are making decisions about response, and the challenges that K–12 stakeholders face in doing so. As this report will make clear, our interviews speak to a variety of strategies and a reliance on a multitude of different partners. We strove to include diverse representation in terms of geographical location and setting as well as school and district size. We also sought to gather input from local as well as state and federal law enforcement agencies and state-level school safety agencies. The next section provides more detail about our literature review, news report analysis, and interview methods.

Methods

Literature Review

We conducted an exploratory literature review between October and December 2022 to identify existing practices for assessing and responding to social media threats and other forms of anonymous threats targeting K–12 schools. We were interested specifically in determining whether there was an existing foundation for work and future guidance in this area. In addition to a focused search of state-level websites related to school safety, we also conducted Google and Google Scholar searches to identify academic and gray literature, news sources, and existing federal- or state-level guidance relevant to threat assessment and response using the following set of key words (we restricted our search to sources published between 2002 and December 2022):

- *social media threat schools*
- *anonymous threat schools*
- *anonymous threat targeted violence schools.*

The relevant sources that were specific to the K–12 education sector included

- nineteen sources in the form of relevant federal- or state-level guidance, covering topics such as digital threat assessment; investigating and managing other types of threats to schools such as bomb threats and swatting incidents; responding to threats, including how to communicate with families and implementing appropriate lockdown procedures; and guidance about social media platforms commonly used by youth
- six pieces of gray literature that discussed trends in social media–based threats and provided loose advice on the steps K–12 schools could take to identify and manage such threats
- six peer-reviewed sources from the academic literature that discuss trends in social media–based threats against schools, steps involved in investigating such threats, and the costs and benefits of strategies and tools designed to monitor student social media and other online content to detect threats
- seventeen news articles detailing recent trends in social media–based threats against K–12 schools and how these have impacted school communities.

To complement this initial search, our exploratory review also sought to identify literature focused on other types of threats that we deemed would hold relevant and translatable lessons for the K–12 school sector. We conducted separate Google and Google Scholar searches for this phase of the review, using the following set of search terms (we also restricted our search to sources published between January 2002 and December 2022):

- *assess* threat written communication*
- *assess* bomb threat*
- *fixated individual*
- *anonymous threatening communication*
- *evaluating threats of violence.*

Most of the literature identified through this secondary search focused on anonymous threats made to public officials, followed by sources addressing anonymous threats from fixated individuals (stalkers), bomb threats, and cyberbullying. An additional set of sources focused on threatening written communications more generally, cyber threats, and general threats of violence. Most of the relevant sources we identified covering these sectors were peer-reviewed publications (17 total), followed by guidance-type documents (4 sources), and gray literature (3 sources). Notably, we identified eight news sources describing trends in "swatting," which, again, are prank calls made to emergency dispatch centers about an ongoing active shooter attack meant to prompt a significant law enforcement response.[1]

Notably, some of the sources identified above also addressed related topics, notably preventing threats via early detection using social media and other monitoring software. These sources and their findings are discussed throughout the report where relevant.

News Reports of Social Media–Based Threat Incidents Against Schools

To identify a sample of news reports of social media–based threats against K–12 schools over a ten-year period from August 2012 to September 2022, we conducted a search on Nexis Uni using the following search terms:

- *social media threats schools.*

Our results returned 1,078 articles from newspapers, newswires, press releases, magazines, and webnews sources.

---

[1] Swatting threats are comparable to social media–based threats due to their anonymous nature and the significant challenges that they introduce around assessing their viability and deciding on the most appropriate response. Like many social media–based threats, they also tend to come in clusters and impact a number of schools across one state or the entire country simultaneously.

The research team reviewed the headline and content of each article to determine whether it included a relevant social media threat incident. We defined a social media threat incident as any instance in which a school received a threat of violence via a social media platform (as opposed to over the phone, by word of mouth, or in written form outside of social media). Threats of violence had to target a specific school or school district, as opposed to a named individual attending or working at a school (e.g., a student or teacher). Articles that did not refer to a specific social media threat incident were excluded from our list; the team eliminated articles that described general trends in school threats (social media–based and other); policies implemented by local education agencies or law enforcement agencies to address threats; threat incidents that did not originate on social media (e.g., threats written on bathroom walls, phoned-in threats); as well as incidents that were otherwise unrelated to social media threat incidents. A total of 791 articles referred to 497 specific social media threats from August 2012 to September 2022.[2]

Having formed this list of 497 incidents from 2012–2022, the research team coded the following variables for each threat incident, based on the information provided in the news articles:

- incident date
- name of targeted school and/or school district
- public or private school
- school education level (e.g., high school)
- social media platform used to make the threat
- school response(s) to threat (e.g., increased police presence)
- whether the local education agency communicated to its community about the incident
- whether the threat was identified as a hoax by law enforcement
- whether the threat was followed by a physical attack
- whether the individual making the threat was identified
- the affiliation of the individual making the threat, if identified (e.g., student, nonstudent)
- school and/or law enforcement action taken against the individual making the threat, if identified.

We also appended demographic information at the local education agency and school level for each incident in our database. Demographic information included urbanicity (e.g., urban, suburban, town/rural), control (public versus private), grades served, enrollment size, student racial/ethnic distribution (e.g., share White students, share Black students, share

---

[2] In some cases, more than one article provided information about the same social media threat. We also came across a number of articles that described social media–based threat incidents targeting a number of different schools across different local education agencies. Given time and resource constraints, we were not able to code every individual incident, especially during time periods when many K–12 schools across the country faced such threats. In these cases, we coded the specific threat about which the news article in question provided the most information.

Hispanic students), and share of students who qualify for free or reduced-priced lunch under the National School Lunch Program (a common proxy for school district poverty level). We obtained these demographic data from the National Center for Education Statistics (NCES). NCES collects these demographic data on all K–12 public schools and public school districts annually in the Common Core of Data (CCD). NCES also collects analogous demographic data on private schools biennially through the Private School Universe Survey. For public schools, we appended CCD demographic data corresponding to the school year in which the social media threat incident occurred. Because data collection on private schools is more scattered and because private schools represent only 2 percent of our sample (and all private school incidents occurred in the 2016–2017 school year or more recently), demographic data for private schools are from the most recent data collection effort, which corresponds to the 2019–2020 school year.

Our analysis of social media threats made against K–12 schools from 2012 to 2022 is exploratory in nature, especially because a large number of threat events is likely to be missing. As noted previously, time and other resource constraints prevented us from collecting systematic information on every social media threat listed in a particular news source. Moreover, it is likely that news coverage of social media threat incidents is biased toward large school districts located in urban and suburban areas. We suspect that this bias stems from two sources. First, these districts are probably more likely to be located in places where there is a local newspaper that can focus attention on these incidents (Grieco, 2019; Simpson, 2019). Second, not only do these districts serve more students (NCES, undated), but incidents of school violence (and threats of violence) tend to be disproportionately concentrated in urban school settings (Wang et al., 2022).

A comparison of our data with national data confirms our dataset is not representative of the national population of K–12 public school districts.[3] As Figure 1.1 shows, districts located in city and suburban settings as defined by the NCES were overrepresented in our sample.

Nevertheless, based on the general literature about social media threats against K–12 schools and what we heard from our interview participants, we believe that our exploratory analysis of a sample of incidents does in fact reflect national trends.

Interviews with K–12 Stakeholders

We selected interview participants via a purposive sampling approach, whereby we sought to include participation across contexts such as geographic location and locale, school district size, and grade levels served. We also sought to include representation from school district-, local-, state-, and federal-level law enforcement organizations, given the often-critical role

---

[3] We caution readers from overinterpreting Figure 1.1. The unit of analyses in our dataset is an *incident*. School districts may be represented multiple times in our data if multiple social media threats occurred in that district over the last ten years. We use the national population of public school *districts* as a reference point because there is no nationally representative dataset of social media *incidents* for us to check our sample against.

FIGURE 1.1

In-Sample School District Urbanicity Compared with National Distribution

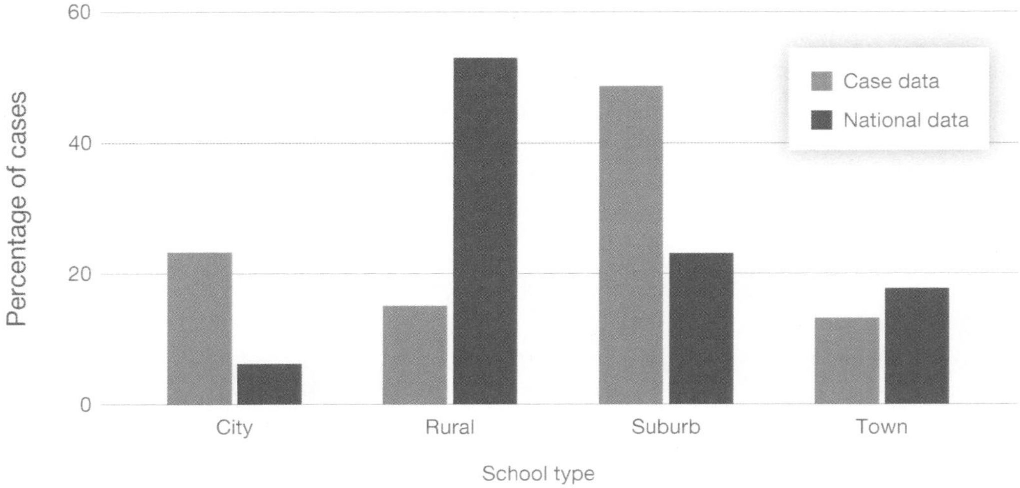

SOURCE: Features Homeland Security Operational Analysis Center (HSOAC) analysis of news reports about social media threats against K–12 schools. For more information, see the discussion of the sourcing approach and methods earlier in this chapter.

that these entities play in assessing social media–based threats of violence and the guidance that they provide to school for responding to them. Between the months of January and March 2023, we conducted a total of 42 interviews with 62 individuals involved in school safety at the federal, state, county, local community, school district, and individual school levels.[4] Our participants represented 17 distinct school districts across 12 U.S. states. All but one of these districts served grades K–12, with one district serving a smaller subset of grades (7–12). NCES categorizes five of these districts as city locales, five as suburb locales, two as town locales, and four as rural. The largest individual district in our sample served more than 400,000 students, and the smallest served fewer than 600 students.

At the state level, we conducted interviews with representatives from state school safety offices, state tip-line directors, and state law enforcement agencies and members of state intelligence fusion centers; a total of 15 states was represented in this set of interviews. At the conclusion of our interviews with state-level personnel, we asked for referrals to individuals in districts in that state who would be willing to speak with us about their approaches to social media–based threats, including processes to assess the viability of threats and make decisions about them. We also reached out to individual districts in areas beyond those represented in our state-level interviews to increase our sample size and make it more geographically representative.

---

[4] All school and school district personnel included in our interview sample were from public schools.

In addition to state-level representatives, we spoke with school district superintendents, school district safety directors, principals and assistant principals, and other district-level personnel such as internet technology directors and communications directors. We also spoke with school resource officers (SROs), SRO supervisors, and members of school district police departments, as well as representatives from municipal law enforcement agencies. At the federal level, we spoke with representatives from agencies tasked with investigating interstate threats, such as personnel from the FBI and the U.S. Department of Homeland Security (DHS). We also spoke with private threat assessment professionals, representatives from county district attorney offices, and individuals from nongovernmental organizations (NGOs) active in threat reporting and assessment. Our final interview sample size was based on saturation (i.e., when no new information surfaced as a result of additional interviews), as well as interviewee responsiveness and availability. Figures 1.2 and 1.3 show the geographies and locales covered in our interviews.

An appendix includes the semistructured interview protocol used for our interviews. During each conversation with our interview participants, we sought to hear about their experiences with social media–based threats as well as the impact that these threats had on their school community. We also asked about processes to assess the viability of received threats, how they made decisions about implementing lockdowns or other

FIGURE 1.2

Geographic Overview of Local Education Agency Interviews

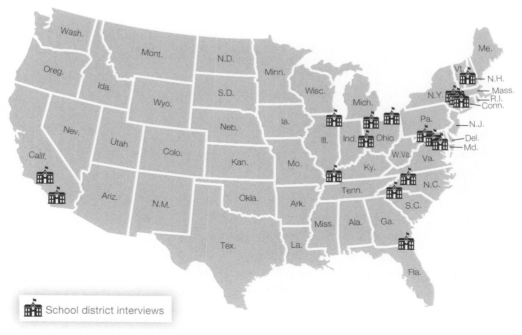

SOURCE: Features HSOAC analysis of K–12 stakeholder interview data.

FIGURE 1.3

Geographic Overview of Other Interviews

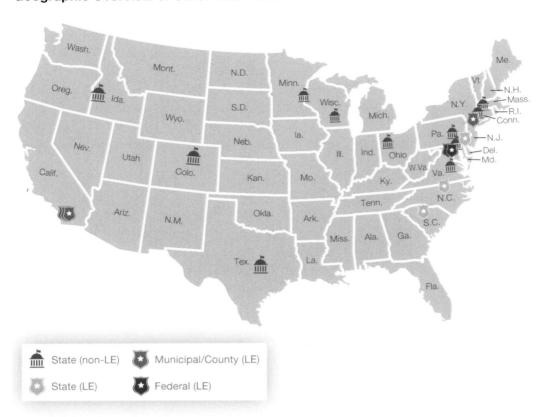

SOURCE: Features HSOAC analysis of K–12 stakeholder interview data.

NOTE: LE = law enforcement. The research team also held one interview with a representative from an NGO, which focused on threat reporting and assessment in K–12 schools. It is not depicted in this figure.

responses, and whether they employed other tools or strategies to detect online threats within their community. We took typed notes during all interviews, which addressed the following topics:

- general trends in threats made against schools via social media platforms
- impact of social media–based threats on K–12 school communities
- processes for assessing threat viability
- partners involved in assessing threat viability
- main challenges to assessing the viability of social media–based threats
- processes for determining appropriate school-level responses
- practices for communicating with the broader school community after receiving a threat
- challenges in deciding on appropriate responses
- practices and tools for detecting social media–based threats.

All interviews were conducted virtually via video- or teleconference, and each one lasted approximately one hour. Each interview was conducted on a voluntary and confidential basis.

We acknowledge several limitations to our study, some of which we have addressed above. First, our sample of social media threat incidents across the country from 2012–2022 is incomplete at best. Given the sheer number of such threats, especially during particular stretches of this time period, time and resource constraints prevented us from capturing and coding every single incident. Many threats also likely go unreported in the media, making the complete picture difficult to track. That said, general news stories about the threats local education agencies face as well as our discussions with a diverse group of K–12 stakeholders across the country suggest that our data captured major trends. Second, though we assess that our interview sample is similarly reflective of nationwide trends and the approaches and challenges that local education agencies face when it comes to social media–based threats of violence, our snowball sampling approach and limits in interviewee responsiveness and availability may exclude some perspectives. Finally, the limited literature on social media threats against K–12 schools precludes us from making definitive judgments about what works best when it comes to assessing the viability of such threats; responding in a way that limits impacts on the school community but still keeps the community safe; and preventing future threats. Our findings are based largely on the experiences of local education agencies and local, state, and federal law enforcement and school safety agencies represented in our interview sample. As local education agencies and their law enforcement partners improve their own practices in dealing with these threats, future research can help further our understanding of what works best.

Organization of This Report

The rest of this report is organized as follows:

- Chapter 2 provides an overview of trends in social media–based threats against schools, including the frequency of threats, their geographical scope, and the impacts that they are having on K–12 communities across the country.
- Chapter 3 describes the steps that local education agencies are taking to investigate the viability of threats received through social media, as well as the challenges that they face in this area.
- Chapter 4 provides an overview of how local education agencies decide how to respond: What considerations lead them to increase law enforcement presence at their schools or activate lock-ins or lockdowns? How do they decide when it is best to close schools in response to a threat? We also outline the various challenges that schools contend with in making these decisions.
- Chapter 5 summarizes our main findings and lays out implications for stakeholders across the K–12 school community.

CHAPTER 2

Trends in Threats Against K–12 Schools

Social media threats are involved in only a small portion of the violent incidents that occur in K–12 schools across the United States. For example, the K–12 School Shooting Database (SSD), which provides a window into school violence that involves firearms, captured 243 incidents of gun violence in or around schools, during the day, on school days in 2022, the last complete year of data (Riedman, 2023).[1] The circumstances of the incidents ranged from neighborhood violence spilling onto school property to violence occurring within the school community—including domestic violence, escalation of conflicts between individual students to potentially deadly force, and even the accidental discharge of firearms authorized to be in the school building (e.g., an SRO's weapon).

It is often difficult to determine whether social media threats or other leakage played a role in individual acts of violence. Information in the media about many school—and non-school—shooting incidents can be sparse, with some incidents receiving only a few para-graphs of attention in a local news report, and little follow-up afterwards. For most shooting incidents, there is no indication that any threatening communications preceded the incident, either via social media or any other means. For some incidents, this is not a surprise: If a gun violence incident escalated from a spontaneous fight between two individuals, the event would be over before there was time for such communications to occur. However, given the ubiquity of social media and electronic communications in students' lives, the reality is that cyberbullying or other virtual conflicts could be a contributor to many incidents without the public ever knowing.

In our review of the 243 shooting incidents included in the SSD for 2022, we identified only eight that could be definitively traced back to some kind of social media activity. Of those, five were related to a TikTok "challenge" seeking to convince students to shoot people at schools with gel-firing pellet guns. The remaining three incidents were associated with more traditional social media threats. One involved threatening posts made by the individual who attacked Robb Elementary School in Uvalde, Texas, in May 2022; another involved a student in Greenville, South Carolina, who shared photos of himself with firearms before carrying out a shooting at his school; and the third involved an adult who shot five people

---

[1] We narrowed our list from the 303 total incidents in 2022 included in the database by eliminating ones that occurred at night, in the evening, or not on a school day to focus most on violence immediately threatening K–12 students.

outside a high school basketball game in connection with an argument about a Facebook post in Milwaukee, Wisconsin.

Analyses of school violence that focus more narrowly on preplanned incidents where communications (including threats made on social media) would be more likely—and the potential benefit of detecting and responding to them more significant—provide a point of comparison. Specifically, one study published by the U.S. Secret Service's (USSS) National Threat Assessment Center (NTAC) focuses on incidents of completed school violence; a companion report examines incidents of averted violence (NTAC, 2019; 2021). Because the time periods covered by each publication differ slightly, with three years of additional data included in the latter publication, any side-by-side comparison of the two is difficult to make.

Nevertheless, we found that a significant portion of both completed and averted attacks at K–12 schools included in the reports were preceded by threatening communications. Depending on how incidents in which the existence of preincident communications is unknown are treated, we calculated that between 66 and 80 percent of completed attacks did in fact include such communication (NTAC, 2019, p. 46). For averted attacks, the findings indicate that 94 percent of the 67 plots included in the analysis were preceded by communications of threat or intent to commit an attack (NTAC, 2021).

Of note, the USSS study of completed attacks found that only "one of the attackers shared his plan via social media," but that individuals associated with 17 additional attacks made "concerning" online posts prior to their attack (NTAC, 2019, pp. 21, 46). Of the incidents of averted school violence examined by USSS, the study finds that in 11 cases "social media played a role in the discovery of the plotters' communications" (NTAC, 2021, p. 25). This suggests between 41 and 56 percent of completed attacks involved some form of online postings and communications, while approximately 16 percent of averted attacks did so as well.

Finally, a RAND study of 600 completed, foiled, and failed mass attacks in the United States from 1995 to 2020 includes a subset of 72 incidents targeting K–12 schools, 53 of which were averted (coded as "foiled" in the database). The remaining 19 incidents were either completed (17) or attempted but failed (2) (Hollywood et al., 2022). This analysis identifies a much smaller portion of completed and failed attacks as having involved communication of threat or intent to do harm before the incident (6 of 19 attacks, or 32 percent). By contrast, 79 percent of averted school attacks included in this study were identified as having involved some form of prior threatening communication (42 of 53 incidents). Across both completed and averted attacks, only nine incidents involved communication on social media or a web forum (three completed/attempted attacks and six averted attacks). Two additional averted incidents are also coded as involving direct electronic communications to individuals. Overall, this corresponds to 16 percent of completed school attacks involving social media or online communications and somewhere between 11 and 15 percent of averted attacks having been preceded by them.

In sum, existing databases of gun violence incidents at K–12 schools suggest that only a small portion was preceded by identifiable social media or other forms of online communications. As a result, developing better ways to assess and respond to threatening communications is only a part of what is needed to protect school communities as many incidents do not involve them. However, both the significant differences that exist between available datasets (summarized in Table 2.1) and difficulties in determining whether social media threats were involved in each incident of violence also suggest the need for caution in how this type of data is used to shape strategy.

Given the reliance on media reports for building violence datasets, it is possible that social media communications have been missed or were not included in press reports of incidents, or in some cases online messages that may have been perceived as threatening in one case were not perceived as such in others. Other communications may have been deleted by individuals planning an attack, fearing that they would lead to their detection. As a result, while we can be certain that some violent incidents are preceded by threats and some are not (e.g., shootings in spontaneous fights among weapon-carrying students), limitations in data create significant uncertainty about many incidents fall into each category.

The differences in the portions of completed and averted incidents involving online communication calculated from different incident datasets also suggest the need for caution. The two main sources examined here have two inclusion criteria, with one focusing on incidents targeting one or more individuals and the other focusing on larger-scale planned attacks. The finding that the percentages of completed incidents involving communication (online and more broadly) calculated from each dataset differ so significantly (Table 2.1) reinforces the challenge schools face: Even with the benefit of hindsight and time to assemble available information about past incidents with known outcomes, the importance of online communications and social media threats is often difficult to determine with certainty. Under the circumstances, the relative frequency of gun violence incidents at K–12 schools and the all-too-common occurrence of mass shootings in general have made social media–based threats especially alarming and forced local education agencies to take most every threat they receive seriously. In what follows, we describe trends in these threats based on our analysis of the literature, interviews with K–12 stakeholders, and a sample of social media–based threats collected from news sources between 2012 and 2022.

TABLE 2.1

Online Communications Preceding Preplanned K–12 School Attacks and Plots

Incidents	Preplanned K–12 Attacks/Plots Targeting 1 or More Individuals[a]		Preplanned K–12 Attacks/Plots Targeting 4 or More Individuals[b]	
	Preincident Communication Identified	Online Communication	Preincident Communication Identified	Online Communication
Completed	66–80%	41–56%	32%	16%
Averted	94%	16%	79%	11–15%

[a] NTAC (2019, 2021).

[b] Hollywood et al. (2022).

The Timing and Targets of Threats Against K–12 Schools

In a survey of 973 K–12 school teachers in October–November 2022, about one-third (35 percent) reported that their school had been disrupted by social media–based threats from students during the 2021–22 school year; more than half of these teachers said that this had happened more than once during that same school year. Teachers in secondary schools—middle and high school levels—were more likely to report disruptions than elementary school teachers (Jackson et al., 2023).

News accounts and other analyses highlight several additional trends in the timing of threats made against schools, such as bomb and shooting threats. Notably, threats made against schools tend to come in cluster patterns, affecting a number of districts across a particular state and sometimes across several states at the same time (Sanchez, Brown, and Gingras, 2022; Santucci, 2022). Indeed, social media–based and other written or phoned-in threats tend to increase during specific times of the school year, such as at the start of the academic year and again in the springtime (Blad, 2022; Santucci, 2022). Clusters of threats received by schools across the country can also be part of so-called social media challenges, such as the December 2021 "National Shoot Up Your School Day" trend on the social media platform TikTok, which encouraged students to bring weapons to school (Stunson, 2021; Taylor, Holpuch, and Cramer, 2021).

Threats, whether they originate on social media or other mediums, also frequently follow high-profile tragedies or coincide with anniversaries of mass school shootings (such as the shooting at Columbine High School in Littleton, Colorado, in April 1999 or at Marjory Stoneman Douglas High School in Parkland, Florida, in February 2018) (Santucci, 2022; Taylor, Hopluch, and Cramer, 2021). One study of threats and incidents of violence at K–12 schools from 2017–2018 found that just over 40 percent of threats made during that school year occurred in the month following the shooting in Parkland, Florida (Klinger and Klinger, 2018).

As described in the previous chapter, we used news articles to identify and analyze 497 individual social media threat incidents targeting K–12 schools from 2012–2022; many of the trends in our sample comport with these copycat and contagion patterns. We identified the largest number of news reports about social media threats during the 2017–2018 school year (133 threats), followed by the 2021–2022 school year (95 threats). This is in line with trends identified in a recent exploratory study of shooting threats made against K–12 schools between the 2018–2019 and 2021–2022 school years, which finds that violent threats increased significantly in 2021–2022 (Peterson et al., 2023). Although our search covered only the first one to two months of the 2022–2023 school year (depending on local education agency start dates), trends suggest that this year is at least on par with the previous year in terms of numbers of threats: In August and September 2022 alone, K–12 schools across the country had already been the target of at least 33 social media–based threats. By comparison, schools seemed to face far fewer threats during the 2019–2020 and 2020–2021 school years, when many local education agencies shifted to remote learning because of the COVID-19 pandemic.

Our sample of threats during this time period suggests that high schools—as opposed to middle and elementary schools—are the most common targets of threats originating on social media. This corroborates findings from a recent study of school shooting threats (Peterson et al., 2023), as well as a fall 2022 survey of K–12 teachers, who reported that disruptive social media threats were more common in secondary schools than in elementary schools (Jackson et al., 2023). Our analysis of news reports also indicates that most incidents targeted schools in suburban locales, followed by city locales. As noted in the previous chapter, however, this distribution may be due to the propensity of news outlets to cover incidents affecting larger local educational facilities in more populated locations rather than incidents in smaller local educational facilities located in sparsely populated rural areas. Moreover, the number of threats identified in specific states largely tracks population size; seven of the top ten states in terms of frequency of social media threat incidents were also among the top ten states in terms of population size (California, Ohio, Pennsylvania, Illinois, Florida, Texas, and Georgia).[2]

Our data also show similar cluster patterns to those discussed above. Specifically, news reports about social media threats suggest that these increase in the aftermath of high-profile mass shootings at schools, such as the Marjory Stoneman Douglas High School shooting in February 2018, the Oxford High School shooting in November 2021, and the Robb Elementary School shooting in May 22. K–12 schools also faced an onslaught of social media threats during the December 2021 TikTok challenge. Figure 2.1 illustrates these trends.

FIGURE 2.1

Timing of Press Reports of Social Media Threats Against Schools, 2012–2022

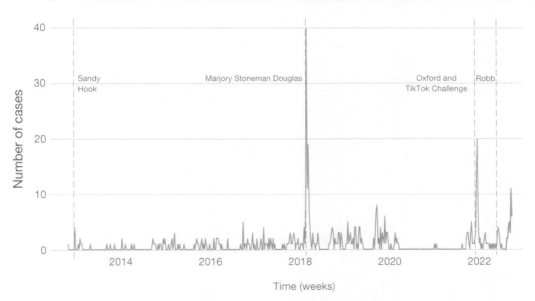

SOURCE: Features HSOAC analysis of news reports about social media threats against K–12 schools. For more information, see the discussion of the sourcing approach and methods in Chapter 1.

---

[2] Peterson et al. (2023) also find that most K–12 schools targeted by threats are high schools, and that threats were more likely at suburban schools between the 2018–2019 and 2021–2022 school years.

Interviews with stakeholders across the K–12 school community also largely confirmed these trends. For example, interviewees noted an upsurge in social media school threats during testing season (e.g., during midterm and final exams) and also in warmer weather, perhaps as part of students' efforts to getting out of school for the day.[3] Interview participants also highlighted that copycat threats of targeted violence were also more common in the aftermath of mass shootings and tended to come in clusters.[4] Many stakeholders from across the country also noticed a spike in social media–based threats after students returned to school following closures related to the COVID-19 pandemic, hypothesizing that social isolation and immersion in various virtual worlds for extended periods might have contributed to what they perceived to be an increase in attention-seeking behaviors.[5]

So-called challenges proliferating across popular social media platforms like TikTok, such as the "Devious Licks," "Sleepy Chicken," "Slap a Teacher," "Missing Child," and "National Shoot Up Your School Day" challenges, also contributed heavily to the clusters of threats received by schools nationwide.[6] Overall, our interviewees confirmed that these "challenge" trends are of great concern not only because of the frequent disruption and stress they impose on the school community, but also due to the costs incurred by local education agencies and their law enforcement partners as they scramble to respond and assess any damage to their facilities.[7]

---

[3] School district representatives from three districts, interviews with the authors, January–March 2023; state-level school safety representative, interview with the authors, February 2023.

[4] Representatives from state school safety agencies in three states, interviews with the authors, February–March 2023; school district representative, interview with the authors, February 2023; county criminal justice representative, interview with the authors, February 2023; federal law enforcement agency representative, interview with the authors, March 2023.

[5] School district representatives from three districts, interviews with the authors, January–February 2023; local law enforcement agency representative, interview with the authors, February 2023; federal law enforcement agency representative, interview with the authors, February 2023.

[6] School district representatives from three districts, interviews with the authors, January–February 2023; representatives from state school safety agencies in four states, interviews with the authors, January–March 2023. On social media challenges, see Wood (2022) and Klein (2022). Various challenges across the TikTok social media platform in particular have called on students to engage in inappropriate and often dangerous behavior at school. For example, the "Devious Licks" challenge, which swept across schools during the 2021–2022 school year, called on students to record themselves stealing something from their schools, resulting in considerable destruction across K–12 campuses nationwide (Klein, 2022). Other challenges have dared kids to consume large doses of Benadryl until they hallucinate, hold their breath until they pass out, or eat chicken cooked in NyQuil (Klein, 2022). The "National Shoot Up Your School" or "School Shooting" challenge that spread across TikTok in December 2021 tasked the platform's users to prank call their schools and local police claiming that there would be an attack on their school on December 17 (Ashworth, 2023).

[7] School district representatives from three districts, interviews with the authors, January–February 2023.

Who Is Making Threats, How Are They Doing So, and What Are They Saying?

Schools receive threats from a variety of mediums, such as notes left somewhere on campus, messages scribbled on bathroom walls, threatening phone calls and emails, and via social media. Many warn of impending school shootings or other acts of mass violence at a specific school, such as bomb threats, while others might target a particular individual or group (Klinger and Klinger, 2018).

Social media is becoming one of the most common sources of threats made against schools: during the 2017–2018 school year, for instance, nearly 40 percent of threats originated on various social platforms (Klinger and Klinger, 2018). The FBI stated in early 2023 that most of the 6,000 threats targeting schools in 2022 were posted to social media (FBI, 2023). In light of statistics showing that 97 percent of teenagers in the United States use the internet daily and that 95 percent of youth between the ages of 13 and 17 report using a social media platform—with one-third reporting they use social media "almost constantly"—these trends are not surprising (Vogels, Gelles-Watnick, and Massarat, 2022; U.S. Surgeon General's Office, 2023; Trump, 2016). They also comport with findings from studies showing that various forms of youth violence, such as gang violence and self-harm, are also occurring more and more in online spaces (Patton et al., 2014). Constant access to technology and the replacement of personal interactions with social media–based ones have moved many elements of youth's lives to the digital realm, including bullying and other harmful behavior (Reynolds et al., 2017). As one of our interview participants noted in reference to the prevalence of these types of threats, "Social media is the new bathroom wall [in schools]."[8]

Social media platforms rise and fall; as certain ones fall out of fashion, others quickly pop up to replace them, often with new features designed to help people connect with broader audiences and what often end up being unknown users (Reynolds et al., 2017). Youth engagement with social media platforms has accordingly shifted over time, with platforms such as Twitter and Facebook falling largely out of favor and others such as Snapchat, TikTok, and Instagram rising to take their place (Vogels, Gelles-Watnick, and Massarat, 2022). These are also the same platforms that K–12 school stakeholders highlight as being common sources of social media–based threats against their communities.[9] Our analysis of a recent sample of news reports about social media–based threats also suggests that students and others are

---

[8] School district representative, interview with the authors, March 2023.

[9] Representatives from state school safety agencies in four states, interviews with the authors, January–March 2023; school district representatives from four districts, interviews with the authors, February and March 2023. News sources provided information on specific social media platforms used to make threats against schools in only 199 of our cases (40 percent of our total sample). In this subset of cases, Snapchat was the most common social media platform used to make threats (95 incidents), followed by Instagram (37 cases), Facebook (19 cases), and TikTok (10 cases).

turning to other sites such as YikYak, After School, and Whisper, which some experts attribute to the additional layer of anonymity granted by these platforms (Trump, 2016).

Many social media–based threats targeting K–12 schools have appeared to be anonymous, at least initially. Accounts linked to threats infrequently identify a student's or other individual's name, making it difficult for local education agencies to know exactly who is posting a threat (see, e.g., CoSN and NSPRA, 2022). Certain platforms, such as YikYak, do not even require users to create profiles or usernames (National Center for Campus Public Safety, 2016). The anonymity that social media platforms afford individuals, as well as their accessibility and ease of use, has likely reduced barriers to making threatening communications in general. A mere handful of clicks on a cell phone can transmit a threat without the social condemnation that might otherwise come with issuing a threat in person (Monagas and Monagas, 2015).

Notably, social media has also made it easier for individuals completely unrelated to a school or local education agency to make eerily specific threats. In 2022, for example, a string of social media–based threats targeted a number of New York City–area schools; law enforcement eventually determined that someone—potentially from overseas—was accessing the names of students via their public Instagram profiles and then posing as a student to threaten well-known schools in the area (Newman and Watkins, 2022). Some individuals will even falsely accuse a student of planning to carry out a school shooting or provide a list of victims. Encryption software and other tactics such as deleting accounts pose especially acute challenges for law enforcement in their attempts to identify the origin of such realistic-sounding threats.

A related and ongoing trend unfolding outside the social media space but affecting local education agencies in similar ways is the so-called swatting phenomenon, whereby an unknown individual phones in false reports of an active shooting or other life-threatening emergency to prompt a massive law enforcement response at a school; the purpose of such calls appears to be to sow panic and fear across a community. Local education agencies across states such as Arkansas, Colorado, Idaho, Florida, Missouri, Texas, and many others have been forced into lockdown situations after receiving calls about shootings in progress at their schools (Blad, 2022). Many of our interview participants also noted the significant challenges that they have faced in relation to swatting incidents since returning to school after COVID-19 closures.[10] Anonymous callers often claim to be inside the targeted building and provide reports of specific classrooms where victims are located. Like social media threats, swatting calls tend to come in clusters, affecting numerous schools across a handful of spe-

---

[10] A total of fourteen interview participants from six different local education agencies and across ten different states specifically referred to their experiences with swatting incidents in our conversations (representatives from state school safety agencies in six states, interviews with the authors, January and February 2023; local law enforcement and criminal justice agency representatives, interviews with the authors, February 2023; school district representatives from five districts, interviews with the authors, January–March 2023.

cific states at the same time; they also sometimes repeat on certain days of the week (see, e.g., Case, 2023). Voice over internet protocol (VoIP) and other technologies make the calls especially difficult to trace, and law enforcement agencies assess that many most likely do not come from within the United States (Yousef, 2022; Jojola and Staeger, 2023).

Despite the initial aura of anonymity, the broader literature on threats against schools and recent trends around the country provides some insight into who may be more likely to engage in threat-making. In the case of social media threats specifically, we heard from our interview participants that most threats are being made by students, as opposed to outsiders;[11] this corroborates findings from other recent analyses of school threats (Klinger and Klinger, 2018). Recent events also seem to suggest that students who are unhappy with school and routinely commit disciplinary offenses, such as skipping school, are some of the more common offenders when it comes to making hoax threats (Santucci, 2022).

Studies of student threat-making also link this behavior to student age as well as demographic and developmental factors (Burnette, Konold, and Cornell, 2020; Cornell and Maeng, 2020). More specifically, a study of student threats of violence across grade levels shows that students tend to make more threats as they get older, but that this trend peaks in the fourth and fifth grades and then drops by the time students reach the tenth grade (Burnette, Konold, and Cornell, 2020). Moreover, most of the threats made by younger students appear impulsive in nature, compared with threats made by older students who may be more prone to carrying out the threat (Burnette, Konold, and Cornell, 2020). Other studies largely corroborate these findings, showing that younger male high school students, minority students, and students in special education are more likely to make school threats (Cornell and Maeng, 2020). Additional studies also show that students who have experienced suspensions, changed schools, or faced legal action were more likely to make substantive threats (Burnette, Datta, and Cornell, 2018).

In our sample of social media threat incidents from 2012–2022, news reports suggest that individuals making what initially appear as anonymous threats are often identified. Across at least 329 incidents during this time period (66 percent of cases), law enforcement agencies were able to identify the individual behind a threat; in over half of these cases (191 incidents), the individual was identified as a student at the targeted school. News reports suggest that most are arrested and charged with a crime.

How Do Schools Become Aware of Threats on Social Media?

K–12 schools become aware of threats in a variety of ways, including via direct communication of a threat by a student, staff, or family member; through formal reporting systems such as tip lines; and via alerts from third-party monitoring programs and software that

---

[11] School district representatives from eight districts, interviews with the authors, January–March 2023; representatives from state school safety agencies in six states, interviews with the authors, February and March 2023.

scan student activity on specific devices (such as school-issued laptops) and school Wi-Fi networks (see, e.g., Moore et al., 2022; Jackson et al., 2023). Approximately three-quarters of teachers surveyed in the fall of 2022 felt confident that threats would be reported if students and staff heard about one (Jackson et al., 2023). Teachers reported that students were most likely to report threats directly to them (87 percent of respondents) or to other school staff members (76 percent); 59 percent of respondents indicated that students were most likely to report threats to school security staff, such as SROs (Jackson et al., 2023). Thirty-one percent of teachers surveyed in the fall of 2022 said that students reported threats through a tip line when they became aware of them (Jackson et al., 2023). Once a school determines that it is the target of a threat, school- and district-level administrators typically coordinate with school-based law enforcement to initiate the investigation process. As we discuss in more detail in Chapter 3, many local education agencies also engage local law enforcement partners to address the threat.

In our interviews of K–12 stakeholders, most told us that they became aware of various threats primarily through direct communication with a school staff member, student, or parent or through an anonymous tip line. In the case of social media threats, students or parents were often the ones to share a screenshot of a concerning post either directly with school staff or via an anonymous reporting platform. For example, a representative from a state-level intelligence fusion center charged with identifying and investigating threats to K–12 schools explained that students often come forward when they see something concerning online; parents often also become aware of students sharing information across diverse platforms and report this activity to school administrators.[12] Some stakeholders also mentioned learning of threats through state- or district-level monitoring software designed to capture specific keywords. As one explained, "[Students] share [information about a threat] either via an adult who lets [the district] know or through our anonymous reporting system. If [students] are online on a device that is supported by our [district] network, [the content] is also flagged thru Gaggle,"[13] which is a safety-oriented school surveillance program.

Indeed, districts' use of technology monitoring services is an emerging trend and one of many efforts to promote school safety (Koumpilova, 2022; Fleury and Dowdy, 2022; Shade and Singh, 2016). These monitoring programs—such as Social Sentinel, Go Guardian, or

---

[12] Federal law enforcement agency representative, interview with the authors, March 2023. Notably, however, one district representative noted that some parents are sometimes uncomfortable reporting a threat to authorities. Instead, they recirculate the threat on social media platforms to make others aware of potential danger. This practice causes additional challenges for investigators, as it is especially difficult to trace a threat back to its original post once it has been posted and reposted numerous times across multiple social media outlets (school district representatives from one district, interviews with the authors, January and February 2023).

[13] School district representative, interview with the authors, February 2023. Gaggle is surveillance software that uses both artificial intelligence and human content moderators to identify "suspicious or harmful" content and images across Google's G-Suite and Microsoft 365 products. It is used primarily by K–12 school districts in the United States (Haskins, 2019).

Gaggle—help identify potential threats preemptively by scanning documents, searches, and social media activity on district-owned devices and devices connected to a district server (O'Leary, 2022). The goal is to flag specific keywords or phrases that are unique to a community (Koumpilova, 2022; National Center for Campus Public Safety, 2016). Though most of our interviewees reported learning about threats via traditional reporting methods, a number also noted local education agencies' use of these types of scanning systems.

However, we identified a number of conflicting views about the utility and effectiveness of such services, both through our interviews and in the emerging literature about the services. As of mid-2022, dozens of colleges and hundreds of K–12 school districts reported using services such as Social Sentinel. However, most did not find the tool useful, largely because the overwhelming majority of flags were false alerts and the services are expensive (Vo and Aldhous, 2019; O'Leary, 2022). Moreover, the proprietary algorithms behind many of these tools make it unclear how they actually work to flag threatening language, and it is unclear whether they introduce racial and other biases (O'Leary, 2022; Schwartz et al., 2022). Interview participants corroborated these findings, emphasizing that while monitoring tools can be useful, especially when it comes to flagging content related to student self-harm or as a source of information to support behavioral threat assessments, their value is at times limited, and alone they are often insufficient when it comes to identifying actual threats. As one representative from a state-level school safety agency explained, "These monitoring tools are useful, but there are multiple other things that need to occur. It's just one spoke of the wheel, and [schools] need other supports and tools as well."[14] Interviewees also highlighted that the software is often expensive and requires significant staff oversight to evaluate each alert that flags specific content. Many district- and state-level stakeholders noted that the demands on school staff can be cumbersome due to the high volume of flagged content; staff are often simply unable to sift through hundreds or thousands of flagged content excerpts daily. As one explained, "[the software] is very overwhelming. . . . Now schools have to dedicate a person to it full time and they just don't have the necessary resources."[15]

The use of such software also introduces significant privacy and other concerns. When students are subject to digital surveillance not only during school hours but also when they are home after school and on weekends and holidays, the practice of using such software carries notable civil rights and privacy implications (Keierleber, 2021). In response, local education agencies have found it critically important to develop clear policies and procedural considerations around the use of such software to protect students' rights and also limit liability. For instance, many have designated specific access and review teams to manage the software and receive alerts, developed audit procedures, and outlined specific steps to take when an alert requires action (National Center for Campus Public Safety, 2016). Moreover, one K–12 stakeholder told us that the practice of constant surveillance blurs the line of when local

---

[14] State-level school safety representative, interview with the authors, February 2023.

[15] State-level school safety representative, interview with the authors, February 2023.

education agencies should be held responsible for not preventing an incident: "There is concern that if schools are publicly committing to monitoring and intervening every time they see something, that is putting a huge amount of responsibility on them and opening them up to blame when incidents do occur."[16]

What Impact Are Threats Having on Schools and Their Broader Communities?

Threats against schools, regardless of their nature, have multiple negative impacts on local education agencies and their communities, ranging from the erosion of trust that schools are safe places to lost instruction time. After receiving a threat, a local education agency's immediate response can include actions to prevent outside access and limit movement inside the school, such lockouts and lockdowns, steps to evacuate all students and staff, or cancel school altogether while an investigation is underway (Newman, 2011; Rich and Cox, 2018).

Indeed, the actions that local education agencies take in response to social media–based threats are typically highly disruptive; they lead to losses in instructional time, impose financial burdens on districts, and often produce fear and stress across the school community (Blad, 2022; FBI, 2018; Newman, 2011; Trump, 2016; Moreschi, 2022; Taylor, Hopluch, and Cramer, 2021; Sanchez, Brown, and Gingras, 2022; Newman and Watkins, 2022). In some rare instances, they have even led to physical injuries (Santana, 2022; Nieto-Munoz, 2019). Lockdowns, school closures, and other responses have not only immediate short-term emotional impact on students, many of whom call and text their parents from their secured classrooms in tears. For a number of children, the trauma of having to stay quiet and take cover inside a dark classroom after a threat is made can be long-lasting and instill fear of returning to school (Rich and Cox, 2018; Perez, 2022). Parents and families are also strongly affected by threats of school shootings. In fact, many will make their own decision to keep their children home from school after hearing about or seeing a social media–based threat, regardless of the school's decision to remain in session as it investigates further (Chabria, 2023; Rich and Cox, 2018). What's more, the very nature of social media and its ability to disseminate information—accurate or not—far and wide at a rapid pace often intensifies the spread of fear. For a school community, the sharing and resharing of threatening social media posts, as well as any associated rumors, further exacerbate the trauma and stress caused by a threat (Wong, 2021; Sanchez, Brown, and Gingras, 2022; Regehr et al., 2017). The media can also play a role in spreading fear and misinformation related to a threat (Regehr et al., 2017).

Social media–based threats against K–12 schools also have a broader impact on community-level resources, most notably on local law enforcement and first responder partners. Through our interviews and analyses of news reports about social media threats,

---

[16] State-level school safety representative, interview with the authors, January 2023.

we found that schools often increase the presence of school security staff and/or local law enforcement officers at a targeted campus in response to a threat; this is often a precautionary measure taken even when a threat is not deemed credible. According to the FBI, social media–based threats not only place police officers and others in unnecessary danger, but also divert critical police resources away from other duties and responsibilities (FBI, 2018). The sheer number of threats that many districts receive, some on a weekly if not daily basis, significantly taxes an already constrained workforce and other resources, especially agencies involved in the initial assessment process (NASRO, 2022; Newman and Watkins, 2022; Taylor, Hopluch, and Cramer, 2021; Wong, 2021; School Safety Grant, 2020; FBI, 2018; Van Brunt, 2016). Both social media–based and swatting threats of active shooter incidents place especially high demands on local community resources, nearly overwhelming local education agency resources as well as law enforcement and first responder personnel (Sanchez, Brown, and Gingras, 2022). Increased law enforcement presence at K–12 schools can also further heighten stress among some K–12 students and staff, compounding what is already a high-stress situation for many (Rich and Cox, 2018).

Our interviewees largely echoed these points, emphasizing the extraordinary resources required to investigate threats and the emotional stress that they place on students, staff, families, and the broader community regardless of whether or not they are real. A number of stakeholders emphasized that threats and ensuing response actions—such as lockdowns—can be especially traumatizing for students who have experienced trauma in the past, whether or not related to school.[17] A local education agency representative noted that "kids are expected to go back to class and go back to learning like [a lockdown] didn't happen. Students have to go through these mental mind shifts all the time—lockdown back to learning. [And in] communities that have had a [gun violence] incident in the past, you are retraumatizing them."[18] Ultimately, recurring threats and associated lockouts, lockdowns, and other responses start to suggest that schools are no longer safe places for children. These impacts last well into the future for many students, parents, and school staff members. For instance, one interview participant described that students and school staff need time to recover from traumatic school events such as threats, and the recovery process can take time away from teaching and learning.[19] Schools located in the same district or in the vicinity of the targeted school also feel these impacts, with many families opting to keep their children home as a precaution.

As we discuss in more detail in subsequent chapters, a number of interview participants also highlighted the significant drain on resources and funds that threats induce. One law enforcement officer employed at a K–12 district explained that "these threats can pull five to ten deputies, equating to 40 manhours just for one complaint [threat]. [There's a] loss of

---

[17] District-, state-, and federal-level school safety stakeholders, interviews with the authors, February–March 2023.

[18] K–12 school district stakeholder, interview with the authors, February 2023.

[19] K–12 school district stakeholder, interview with the authors, February 2023.

learning, sometimes an evacuation and weapons searches—all of this can take multiple hours depending on the threat, and then you have to consider the additional costs to the district and need to pull staff."[20] Other interview participants noted that when police divert significant resources to a targeted school, other areas in the community are less protected from crime and everyday risks: "There are agencies for miles that respond. You are taking police officers off the streets, sheriff deputies out of the counties, and they all converge."[21]

---

[20] K–12 school district stakeholder, interview with the authors, January 2023.

[21] State-level school safety agency representative, interview with the authors, March 2023.

CHAPTER 3

Assessing the Credibility of Threats

Given the rising number of threats made against schools nationally, assessing the viability of each one is a daunting and resource-intensive task. As of this writing, few resources, studies, or other materials provide robust guidance for how to assess the credibility of social media–based threats, many of which are anonymous and not immediately linkable to a specific individual. In this chapter, we draw on a review of the literature about assessing threats—particularly written communications but also other types of anonymous threats—as well as interviews with stakeholders across the K–12 community to understand the steps, processes, and partners involved in assessing the credibility of social media–based threats against schools, as well as the challenges that local education agencies and other stakeholders face in trying to do so.

The Literature and Existing Guidance on Assessing Threat Credibility

One of the most significant challenges that local education agencies face when they are the target of a social media threat is distinguishing between posts that are seeking attention or a reaction and those that pose an actual threat to their communities. In an ideal situation in which a threatening individual's identity is known, a behavioral threat assessment would consider the threat in context, taking into account factors such as previous social media activity and other behavior (Van Brunt, Lewis, and Solomon, 2021, p. 66). But since social media threats are often anonymous, how can local education agencies evaluate the credibility of such threats?

Common Indicators of Credibility in Threatening Communications

Studies point to a number of indicators that help assess risk in threatening communications, whether these are verbally transmitted, posted to social media, sent via email or a hand-written letter, or submitted to a threat-reporting platform. Across various settings, including K–12 schools, higher education, workplaces, and the broader community more generally, we found that common indicators, or "flags," of elevated risk fall into the following categories (Mitchell and Palk, 2016; Simons and Tunkel, 2014; Amman et al., 2017):

- identified motive behind a threat
- feasibility of the threatened action
- escalatory actions taken
- warning behaviors exhibited by the threatening individual.

Most of the studies included in our review presume that the identity of a threatening individual is known. In a review of the threat assessment research literature across diverse domains, researchers identified common areas of inquiry that have proved useful in assessing violence risk from a variety of threats, be they threats of workplace violence, school-based threats, or threats against public figures (Mitchell and Palk, 2016). Specifically, factors such as a threatener's mental wellness, evidence of preparation or access to weapons, details about specific motivations for an attack, and risk behaviors such as a history of substance use or abuse often add weight to a specific threat (Mitchell and Palk, 2016).

The FBI's Behavioral Analysis Unit also notes that specific details included in a threat—such as personal information about a targeted individual or detail about specific weapons and intended violent actions—can elevate concern (Amman et al., 2017). Hints of physical proximity to a target, such as geolocation, also add weight to a threat, as can the use of escalatory language, repeated communication, and evidence that the threatening individual has access to a weapon, such as a photo of an individual posing with a rifle (Van Brunt, 2016; Amman et al., 2017).

The mode of threatening communication might also provide hints about a threat's viability. In a study of 77 Finnish adolescents under psychiatric evaluation, researchers found that those who made online threats (e.g., via email or another virtual medium) were more likely to have made preparations to actually carry out their attack compared with adolescents who made more impulsive, offline threats (Lindberg et al., 2012). Other studies suggest that individuals who send threats to public officials via email, as opposed to physical letters, are more likely to engage in violence against their target than letter writers are (Schoeneman-Morris et al., 2007).

Recent studies of averted school shootings largely confirm the relevance of many of these risk indicators for school-based threats. An analysis of 82 incidents of averted mass violence in K–12 schools found that most would-be attackers engaged in detailed planning prior to their intended attack, for instance, by conducting internet searches for bomb-making instructions or gathering details about assault weapons and other gear used in past mass attacks (Cowan et al., 2022). Many also developed lists of specific individuals to target during the attack and demonstrated an interest in previous mass violence incidents (Cowan et al., 2022). A review of more than 844 K–12 threat cases from 339 schools using the Comprehensive School Threat Assessment Guidelines model also found that threats were more likely to be deemed "substantive" when accompanied by a prior history of violence on the part of the threatening individual, when the threatening student had access to a weapon, or when the threat also involved communications of self-harm (Van Brunt, Lewis, and Solomon 2021, p. 89; Cornell and Maeng, 2020). Passionate references to past injustices and references to previous mass attackers have also all been identified as "significant aggravating elements" in assessments of student written communications (Van Brunt, Lewis, and Solomon, 2021, p. 89).

Assessing Anonymous and Social Media Threats

Anonymous threats pose unique challenges insofar as the characteristics and motivations of the threatening individual are unknown. Anonymity also often compounds a victim's fear and apprehension (Van der Vegt et al., 2022). While many of the indicators specified above may also be useful in assessing the imminent risk posed by an anonymous threat, assessing the risk potential of anonymous threats posted to social media is especially difficult (Simons and Tunkel, 2014; Newman, 2011; National Center for Campus Public Safety, 2016). Many social media platforms allow users to create fake accounts or post content anonymously (Trump, 2016; Amman et al., 2017), and the reposting of content by multiple users makes it more difficult and time consuming to identify the original source of a threat (Moreschi, 2022; Regehr et al., 2017). In some cases, tracing the origins of social media threats is simply unfeasible if social media companies remove threatening content as well as the user account associated with that content.

Moreover, certain trends in the use of social media to issue threats create new challenges for both local education agencies and law enforcement. While specificity has traditionally been an indicator of heightened violence risk in other forms of threatening written communications (Van Brunt, 2016), hoax threateners can fairly easily find details about specific school districts, individual schools, and sometimes individual students online (Newman and Watkins, 2022) and can therefore make their threats appear more convincing. Encryption software has also made it considerably more difficult for law enforcement agencies to trace the origins of threats (Newman and Watkins, 2022; Wong, 2021).[1]

In response to swatting calls targeting K–12 schools, which pose many of the same challenges as anonymous social media–based threats, law enforcement agencies have highlighted that 911 dispatch centers are typically inundated with calls about an active shooter during an actual emergency. Receiving just one call about a shooting in progress is therefore often an indicator of a hoax threat (NASRO, 2022). With respect to social media threats specifically, clusters of threats targeting schools in different geographical locations within or across states are also likely an indication of hoaxes. When a number of schools across the United States received an onslaught of threats in September 2022, law enforcement agencies noted that "waves of false alarms are often the work of disgruntled pranksters trying to disrupt school" and that these hoaxes tend to increase at certain times during the school year (Santucci, 2022).

Still, law enforcement personnel who have responded to the growing number of social media threats against schools report that making generalizations about these threats is difficult, given the unique characteristics of each one (Desai, 2022). Pinpointing the specific

---

[1]   Swatters in particular have become savvy when it comes to using technology such as VoIP and computer-generated voices to mask their identities and locations (Cox, 2023).

individual who posted a threat can be a time-consuming process that depends on accessibility of information from a social media site. What's more, the situation is often complicated when vague threats such as those including just the initials of a school (e.g., "GHS") spread on social media across various locales; determining which "GHS" is the target of the threat often requires an "all-hands-on-deck" response (Desai, 2022).

Table 3.1 summarizes common categories of threat indicators from across various literature domains on threatening communication, including anonymous threats.

TABLE 3.1

Indicators to Assess Threatening Communication Referenced in the Literature

Category	Indicator	Literature Focus					
		Social Media Threats: School Settings	Written Threats: Non-School Settings	Bomb Threats	Communication by Fixated Individuals	Threats to Public Officials	K–12 Behavioral Threat Assessment
Motive	Prior relationship to or grievance against target; personalized motive	✓	✓	✓	✓		✓
Motive	Personalized language	✓	✓			✓	
Feasibility	Names of targets, time, place, methods	✓	✓	✓		✓	✓
Feasibility	Physical proximity to target/expressed intent to approach	✓			✓	✓	✓
Feasibility	Access to resources, materials to carry out threat (e.g., weapons)	✓		✓	✓	✓	✓
Feasibility	Evidence of planning (e.g., research, preparation)	✓	✓	✓	✓	✓	✓
Escalation	History of threats	✓	✓	✓		✓	✓
Escalation	Increase in length and frequency of contact	✓			✓	✓	✓
Warning Behavior	Warrior, commando mentality	✓	✓		✓		
Warning Behavior	Identification with previous mass attackers	✓	✓		✓		✓
Warning Behavior	"othering"/references to out-group (us, them, they)	✓	✓				

SOURCES: Adapted from Amman et al. (2017); Burnette, Datta, Cornell, 2018; Cornell (2003); Cornell and Maeng (2020); Cowan et al. (2022); Dwyer and Osher (2020); Meloy (2014); Meloy et al. (2012); Milkovich (2020); Mitchell and Palk (2016); Monagas and Monagas (2015); Mullen et al. (2009); Newman (2011); NTAC (2019); Regehr et al. (2017); Safer Schools Together (undated-a, undated-b); Schoeneman et al. (2011); Schoeneman-Morris et al. (2007); Shrestha, Akrami, and Kaati (2020); Trump (undated); Tunkel (2002); Van Brunt (2016); Van Brunt, Lewis, and Solomon (2021); Van der Vegt et al. (2022); Winer and Halgin (2016).

Strategies for Assessing the Credibility of Social Media Threats

Our interviewees echoed many of these insights when we asked them about strategies that they use to investigate threats against K–12 schools originating on social media. When social media threats were not anonymous (e.g., when a student posted an identifiable photo of themselves with a weapon or made a threat from an identifiable account), schools could apply traditional threat assessment practices to assessing a student's risk potential, including engaging law enforcement partners to conduct home visits to identify any potential access to weapons.[2] With respect to anonymous threats, however, assessing credibility and violence risk was less straightforward. Interviewees described how they adapted existing threat assessment criteria and practices, but also told us about additional indicators that helped them determine the level of concern a threat actually posed.

Table 3.2 summarizes the categories of factors identified over the course of our interviews with local education agency representatives, state school safety agencies, and personnel from various local, state, and federal law enforcement agencies. The table expands on the structure of Table 3.1, elaborating on various assessment categories and indicators of concern to account for anonymous social media threat assessment practices as described by our interviewees. Speaking to the difficulty of assessing anonymous threats, stakeholders across the K–12 community described both factors that increased the perceived credibility of a threat and those that degraded credibility and suggested a threat might in fact be a hoax. Notably, nearly all of our interview participants emphasized that a threat against a school must initially be taken at face value (i.e., deemed credible) with initial assessment of factors like those in Table 3.2 driving judgments about how serious and how immediate the threat appears. Through an ensuing investigation and threat assessment process, local education agencies and their law enforcement partners then look for flags indicating that the threat is *not* credible.

We also asked our interview participants to describe the *process* of assessing a threat's viability. Through our conversations with representatives from local education agencies and various law enforcement agencies, we learned that common first steps include tracing the internet protocol (IP) address from which a threat was made. While anonymity will typically slow down the process of identifying the origin of a threat, local education agencies are usually able to do so with assistance from law enforcement partners and social media companies.[3] Once an IP address is identified, it can usually be linked back to an individual or specific location. In cases where schools received a threat from an IP address located in a different state or in an entirely different country, this often reduced the weight of that threat

---

[2] School district representatives from three districts, interviews with the authors, January and February 2023; local law enforcement agency representative, interview with the authors, February 2023.

[3] School district representatives from two districts, interviews with the authors, January and February 2023; representatives from state school safety agencies in three states, interviews with the authors, January and February 2023.

TABLE 3.2

Factors Cited by Interviewees in the Assessment of Social Media Threats

Category	Risk Indicator	Notes for Application to Assessing Social Media Threats	Effect on Assessed Risk	Frequency Cited by Interviewees
Motive	Prior relationship to or grievance against target; personalized motive	• Mentions of specific individuals or locations can suggest prior relationship or grievance, but public information can be used in an effort to increase perceived credibility of hoax threats. Indicators of gang affiliation can suggest grievance in even anonymous threats. • Seeking to connect what appeared to be anonymous threats to individual circumstances at school (e.g., a problematic individual recently expelled from school) helped support assessment.	Increase	Medium
	Personalized language	• Mentions of specific names and other personally identifiable information was flagged as concerning, though if such information is publicly available it could be used in hoax threats.	Increase	Low
Feasibility	Names of targets, time, place	• As with motive, interviews cited mentions of specific individuals as targets as a risk indicator. Specific target locations and planned attack times (versus vague suggestions of a future attack) were also cited.	Increase	High
	Methods, *outcomes*	• Specificity about weapon type and particular tactics, as well as a detailed focus on the scale or scope of the outcomes (e.g., body count), was an indicator of concern even in anonymous threats. A smaller subset of interviewees cited expressions of suicidal intent in a threat as particularly concerning.	Increase	Medium
Feasibility	Physical proximity to target/ expressed intent to approach			High
		• Because social media threats and swatting calls are frequently made at a distance from the targeted school (e.g., from abroad), indicators that suggested that the threatener is in actual physical proximity of the school would add weigh to a threat. Examples included transmission of a threat on the school network through short range modes such as Bluetooth sharing (e.g., Apple's Airdrop function). Metadata analysis of photos suggesting that they were taken recently, livestreaming tactics, availability of geolocation data, and any local information included in the threats that is not readily available online also added weight to a threat.	Increase	

Table 3.2—Continued

Category	Risk Indicator	Notes for Application to Assessing Social Media Threats	Effect on Assessed Risk	Frequency Cited by Interviewees
		• Conversely, a number of analytic approaches can raise doubts that a threatener is local to the school. These include analysis of IP addresses or other metadata related to the threat, incorrect information cited in a threat (e.g., nonexistent classroom numbers), or indicators suggesting that the threat is coming from abroad (e.g., foreign accents for called-in threats; spelling or grammatical errors in written threats).	Decrease	
	Access to resources, materials to carry out threat (e.g., weapons)			High
		• Photos of weapons or statements emphasizing access to weapons by the individual making the threat raise concern.	Increase	
		• Evidence suggesting that photos of weapons used in threat are internet stock images or reused from past or current threats in other locations suggest the threat is a hoax.	Decrease	
	Evidence of planning	• Although evidence of planning an actual violent incident is key in standard threat assessment protocols, application to anonymous threats is more difficult (e.g., it would only be relevant in a situation in which an anonymous social media poster shared information over time suggesting preparation for an attack).	Increase	Low
Escalation	History of threats/ increasing length or frequency of communications	• In traditional threat assessments, whether threats made by an individual have increased in seriousness over time and whether the individual has made repeated threats are important factors in assessing violence risk. For anonymous and social media threats, the role of escalation and repetition is more difficult to assess. If the identity of the threatener is not known, these factors can only be assessed only at the level of the online account from which the threat was made (and it may have been created in the recent past in an effort to maintain anonymity).[a] As a result, how threats are changing over time or repetition of threats may be more difficult to distinguish and evaluate for social media–based threats.	Increase	Medium

Table 3.2—Continued

Category	Risk Indicator	Notes for Application to Assessing Social Media Threats	Effect on Assessed Risk	Frequency Cited by Interviewees
Warning behavior	Warrior, commando mentality	• In online threats, the traditional risk factor of a "warrior or commando mentality" overlaps with information that would suggest access to weapons (discussed above). As a result, photos of an individual with weapons and extreme language related to violence or tactics would also relate to this standard risk factor.	Increase	Medium
	Identification with previous mass attackers	• Numerous interviewees emphasized that identification with previous school shooters (e.g., the perpetrators of the Columbine attack in particular) was a significant warning sign of potential violence.	Increase	Medium
	"Othering"/ references to out-group (us, them, they)	• This factor was not flagged by interviewees with respect to individuals at risk of perpetrating school violence.		
Uniqueness	*Multiple schools or school districts receiving similar threats at the same time*	• When multiple schools in an area receive similar threats at or near the same time, the level of concern and credibility of each individual threat is reduced.	Decrease	Medium
	Recycling of previous threatening materials	• With screen captures and other examples of previous threats available online, threateners—particularly hoax threateners—may simply reuse or repost old threats.	Decrease	Low
Timing	*Recent violent incidents at other schools*	• Interviewees cited proximity in time to other incidents of school violence as a complex risk factor. Experience has shown both pulses of hoax threats after violent incidents, but past incidents can also be triggers for copycat violence.	Ambiguous	Low
Language	*Apparent immaturity of threatener*	• Because violent incidents are more frequently carried out by older students, language indicators that suggest the source of a threat is very young reduce concern.	Decrease	Medium
	Apparent legal awareness of threatener	• When a threat appears to be crafted such that the threat itself is not legally actionable (i.e., staying below thresholds for implied imminent violence), there is increased concern about the intention of the individual to follow through on the threat.	Increase	Low

Table 3.2—Continued

Category	Risk Indicator	Notes for Application to Assessing Social Media Threats	Effect on Assessed Risk	Frequency Cited by Interviewees
	Apparent native language of threatener	• Given the frequency of threats transmitted from abroad, interviewees indicated that if the threat suggested English was not the source's first language that could reduce concern. However, this indicator would be less relevant for schools serving multilingual communities.	Decrease	Low
Audience	*Reporting sources*	• Indications that a threat has been transmitted broadly (e.g., multiple independent reports of the threat from students and members of the community) and transmission through social media streams with significant numbers of followers were flagged as concerning.	Increase	Medium
	Platform	• If a threat is posted on a social media platform that is not routinely used by the apparent source (e.g., a threat supposedly from a student but posted on Facebook), credibility is reduced.	Decrease	Low

SOURCE: Features HSOAC analysis of interviews with local education agency personnel, representatives from state school safety agencies, and local, state, and federal law enforcement agency representatives.

NOTE: Risk indicators that were identified in interviews as specific to social media (versus being analogous to factors identified from the literature on assessment of other threats) are indicated in blue italic type. Not all interviewees cited specific risk factors in our discussions about assessment of social media–based threats. The frequency column provides a qualitative measure of how frequently each of the factors was cited during our interviews: "low" frequency indicates the factor was mentioned by 1–4 interviewees; "medium" frequency indicates the factor was mentioned by 5–10 interviewees; and "high" frequency indicates the factor was mentioned by more than 10 interviewees.

[a] One interviewee mentioned specifically that with children, transmission of a threat to more people (e.g., initially 10 and then 25 later) should not be considered escalation but rather was more likely to reflect attention-seeking behavior.

and allowed a school to return to near-normal operations.[4] Involving social media companies in the threat investigation process has additional benefits: They can freeze user accounts and preserve social media content for use during an investigation, and they can also help identify actual names behind so-called vanity accounts.[5] Other stakeholders did note some difficulties in engaging social media companies, however, especially insofar as obtaining warrants can be a slow process in situations when time is of the essence.[6]

---

[4] Representatives from state law enforcement agencies in two states, interviews with the authors, February 2023.

[5] State law enforcement agency representative, interview with the authors, March 2023; school district representative, interview with the authors, February 2023; county criminal justice representative, interview with the authors, February 2023; local law enforcement agency representative, interview with the authors, February 2023.

[6] School district representatives from two districts, interviews with the authors, February and March 2023; state-level school safety agency representative, interview with the authors, February 2023.

Another important part of the investigation process involves looking into trends developing in a threatening social media post and speaking with students. Local education agency representatives, including SROs and other school police personnel, told us that they can look to statistics such as who "liked" a post or at a list of account followers to help discern the origin of a threat. Direct contact with students is also important. One school-based law enforcement officer, for instance, emphasized that his networks inside the school and relationships with students were key to investigating threats: "I have a group of kids [I can rely on]. A lot of times they come to me with things. Or I can ask them questions. These relationships with a network of students are key to the SRO role—they really help us out."[7]

Our interview participants also described some of the steps they took and tools they used to assess specific content in a social media threat, such as photos. A number of interview participants from local education and law enforcement agencies spoke to the value of reverse image searches in particular, which can help identify stock or recycled photos and images.[8] A number of states maintain databases of images used in previous social media threats across the state or even nationally, and this has helped local education agencies and their law enforcement partners quickly discern whether a threat is less likely to be credible.[9] Local education agencies and local law enforcement agencies also commonly reach out directly to neighboring districts and agencies for additional intelligence about a threat, such as asking whether they, too, have been the target of a similar or identical social media post. As noted, threats containing recycled content, such as threats spreading across the country in response to TikTok challenges or threats targeting multiple schools in clusters on the same day, suggest that they are hoaxes.

Key Partners in Assessing the Viability of Threats

As the preceding section highlights, local education agencies work with a number of partners to assess the level of risk posed by a threat. First and foremost, a common refrain in both news coverage of social media–based threats and our discussions with interview participants was that school administrators are not trained investigators and do not have experience in investigation tactics. As one expert noted in response to the overwhelming number of threats received by schools during the December 2021 TikTok challenge, "[Schools] are not investigative bodies; they are trying to educate children" (Taylor, Holpuch, and Cramer, 2021).

---

[7] School district representative, interview with the authors, February 2023.

[8] Representatives from state-level school safety agencies in three states, interviews with the authors, January and February 2023; school district representatives from two districts, interviews with the authors, January 2023; local law enforcement agency representative, February 2023.

[9] School district representative, interview with the authors, February 2023; state-level school safety agency representative, interview with the authors, February 2023.

Our interview participants largely agreed. One interviewee from a state-level law enforcement agency, for instance, told us that "most schools don't have the capability to identify the source of a threat and assess its viability. There is a lot of reliance on the SRO and the [law enforcement] agency the SRO comes from, but most [local education agencies] do not have a proactive threat assessment capability."[10] Other stakeholders from different states expressed similar opinions and added that "the level of training for school staff isn't matching up with the changing way threats are made."[11]

Indeed, a notable additional challenge for individuals and organizations involved in the assessment of social media threats is the reality that social media platforms are numerous and dynamic and that those that are popular among youth today might not be so tomorrow (Amman et al., 2017; Reynolds et al., 2017). Students are often more versed in the specifics of particular social media platforms than the adults responsible for conducting investigations of social media threats (Amman et al., 2017). As a result, interview participants noted that the expertise needed to assess threats posted across social media platforms is difficult to maintain: "It is challenging to stay on top of the trends. [Social media] is a constantly changing field."[12]

Given these challenges, many local education agency representatives who participated in our interviews stressed the importance of engaging with law enforcement and other partners such as social media companies to assess the credibility of social media–based threats. These views also reflect best practices found in the threat assessment literature; a number of studies emphasize the value of multidisciplinary teams to school violence prevention efforts more generally and stress the importance of collaboration between schools and law enforcement (Cornell and Maeng, 2020; Raeger et al., 2017; Van Brunt, Lewis, and Solomon, 2021; NTAC, 2018, 2019; NASRO, 2022; Trump, undated; Amman et al., 2017).[13] In the case of social media–based threats specifically, the little guidance that exists also points to the value of additional resources beyond law enforcement, such as experts with deeper knowledge of emerging technologies who can help assess anonymous online content in particular (U.S. Department of Homeland Security, 2021; Amman et al., 2017).

The states and districts represented in our interview sample varied in their approaches to involving local and other partners in threat assessment. For example, while some districts seek support from local law enforcement immediately after receiving a threat, others involve them only after having done their own due diligence and investigating. As one state school safety representative noted, "I have heard from some districts that if they have any threats, they defer immediately to law enforcement and wait to be informed about next steps. Some

---

[10] State law enforcement agency representative, interview with the authors, February 2023.

[11] State-level school safety agency representative, interview with the authors, February 2023.

[12] State-level school safety agency representative, interview with the authors, February 2023.

[13] Guidance specific to digital threat assessment in schools recommends informing law enforcement of an online threat as a key first step in the investigation process (Safer Schools Together, undated-b); Illinois Terrorism Task Force School Safety Working Group, 2018b).

districts minimally reach out to law enforcement, they mainly try to vet [reported threats] themselves, and if there is [something credible], they will bring in law enforcement in a limited capacity."[14]

Overall, our interview discussions pointed to the value of engaging local law enforcement partners in an area where local education agencies are often at a loss. One stakeholder, for instance, told us that "schools are scared to make the decisions. . . . It is outside of their wheelhouse to assess credibility and figure out the response [to a threat], so they bring in law enforcement."[15] In many cases, the critical link between a local education agency and a local police department is the school or district SRO. Other local education agency staff, such as an assistant principal, principal, superintendent, among others, can also build strong rapport with local law enforcement and serve as the main liaison.[16] Generally speaking, longstanding relationships with local law enforcement partners help to build trust. For a number of local education agencies in our interview sample, having a specific liaison in a police department or having law enforcement personnel regularly check in with their schools reassured them that someone with the right expertise was available to help investigate a threat and make timely decisions to keep their community safe.[17] Some law enforcement agencies also have technology units that have proven especially valuable in the investigation of internet-based anonymous threats.[18] In addition, representatives from school district police departments described how their officers often seek input directly from trusted students or younger school staff when investigating social media–based threats; individuals who regularly use social media can help decode slang and identify specific modes of interaction common among youth (e.g., the existence of hidden "rooms" within a specific social media platform).

Despite consensus about the importance of local education agency and law enforcement collaboration when it comes to assessing the viability of social media threats, we did identify some variation in the extent to such collaboration was possible. Some representatives from state school safety agencies, for instance, noted that rural school districts do not always have consistent access to the same resources as urban districts; many rural locales have smaller, less well-resourced police departments compared with suburban and urban locales, which can impact the timeliness of the assistance they are able to offer schools facing a threat.[19] Representatives from federal law enforcement agencies also highlighted that there can be significant variation in the capabilities of different school district police departments and

---

[14] State-level school safety representative, interview with the authors, February 2023.

[15] State-level school safety representative, interview with the authors, March 2023.

[16] School district representative, interview with the authors, January 2023.

[17] School district representatives from six districts, interviews with the authors, January and February 2023; state law enforcement agency representative, interview with the authors, February 2023; state-level school safety agency representative, interview with the authors, February 2023.

[18] School district representative, interview with the authors, February 2023.

[19] Representatives from state-level school safety agencies in two states, interviews with the authors, February 2023.

individuals within those departments: "Some areas have amazing SRO programs. These officers have great relationships with the students; they know how to ask questions that let them sort out whether a threat is real or not. But there is no SRO standard across the country. Some are just there, and other schools are served by patrol officers who know nothing about a school."[20] Different community attitudes toward police in schools, especially after national conversations to reduce police presence in schools in summer 2020 (see, e.g., Cowan, Hubler, and Taylor, 2021), have also impacted the extent to which local education agencies included in our interview sample engaged with law enforcement on a variety of school safety issues.[21]

Conclusion

Assessing the credibility of an anonymous threat posted to social media is a challenging undertaking for local education agencies, which often lack the relevant expertise and capabilities to do so. Nevertheless, our review of relevant literature about written threatening communications, as well as interviews with a diverse set of stakeholders working in or with the K–12 community to address these threats, has provided useful insight.

Studies of and guidance for assessing risk in threatening communications highlights some indicators. Language indicative of a personal grievance or motive for violence, as well as hints of an impending attack's increased feasibility—such as access to a weapon, specific details about a target, or evidence of planning—often add weight to a threat. Repeated threatening communications are often evidence of escalation, and references to prior mass attacks or attackers might also elevate concern about a particular threat.

Our interviews with local education agencies, law enforcement agencies, and school safety stakeholders suggest that these are also useful indicators when it comes to assessing the violence risk of social media threats specifically. But interview participants also pointed to additional clues that helped them discern between hoax and real threats on various virtual platforms. The specificity of a threat may or may not be an indicator. In today's age of social media and given the ease of accessing information on the internet, it is fairly easy for complete strangers to gather eerily specific information about a school or even particular students. Even hoax threats, in other words, can sound targeted and specific. Instead, a more valuable clue might be the timing of a threat. Local education agencies' experiences with social media threats over the last several years have suggested that they tend to come in clusters and that these cluster patterns are often indicative of hoaxes. The days and weeks following mass shootings as U.S. schools are often rife with threats, and so-called challenges across various social media platforms also often prompt noncredible threats that schools must nevertheless take seriously.

---

[20] Federal law enforcement agency representative, interview with the authors, February 2023.

[21] School district representatives from two districts, interviews with the authors, February 2023; state-level school safety agency representative, interview with the authors, February 2023.

We also learned about the importance of collaboration between local education agencies and local law enforcement agencies in addressing social media threats. School administrators, teachers, and other school staff understandably are not investigators—nor should we be asking them to become investigators. Instead, relationships built up over time with local police or sheriff's departments can ensure that local education agencies have access to the capabilities and resources required to adequately assess a threat. In turn, local law enforcement agencies greatly benefit from the deep knowledge that school administrators, teachers, and other staff have of their school community. In this regard, SROs and school police officers have a unique role to play in assessing the viability of threats. When they are trusted by the student body and by school staff, their networks inside the school and ties to law enforcement agencies outside the school make them a key asset in the threat investigation process.

CHAPTER 4

Responding to Threats

According to a *Washington Post* analysis, a school somewhere in the United States went into lockdown every school day between early September 2017 and late May 2018, due either to gun violence or what was often an anonymous yet seldom legitimate threat of violence (Rich and Cox, 2018). Threats of violence force local education agencies to make decisions about how best to keep their school community safe while investigating the viability of those threats. As the preceding chapter indicates, local education agencies often treat every threat as initially credible; this means that they must assess each one and then decide on the appropriate response. Whatever the circumstances of a threat, deciding how to respond is difficult. Many response options have negative impacts on teaching and learning and can be emotionally stressful for students, school staff, and families. Our interview participants pointed to other considerations that often factor into the decisionmaking process, such as whether a local education agency has enough busses to transport students to reunification areas or whether a school has enough lunches to feed all students in the case of a lockout in which no one is allowed to leave campus. Local education agencies are especially challenged when it comes to implementing a balanced response—one that demonstrates to the broader community that schools have the safety and security of teachers, students, and staff first and foremost on their mind, but also avoids overly disrupting teaching and learning and potentially aggravating already stressful and traumatic situations. In the words of one of the experts consulted during this work, "You can't get an Instagram threat and put your kids under desks." In this chapter, we draw on our analysis of recent data on social media–based threats against K–12 schools, existing literature, and our interviews with K–12 school stakeholders to illustrate how local education agencies have been responding to social media–based threats, as well as the challenges they face in doing so.

Deciding on the Appropriate Response

During the 2021 TikTok challenge calling on students to "shoot up your school," schools across the country either closed, added security, or implemented other responses to keep their communities safe. According to news reports, local education agencies in at least six states made the decision to close; but some of the largest districts in the country decided to stay open. Instead of shutting their doors, they notified their communities that they were taking warnings about the social media challenge seriously and monitoring rumors. Many also increased police presence at their schools or asked students to leave their backpacks at home that day (Taylor, Hopluch, and Cramer, 2021).

Indeed, our review of a sample of social media–based threats targeting K–12 schools from 2012 to 2022 suggests that local education agencies have a range of response options available to them when they are the target of threatening communications. We were able to identify school- or local education agency-level responses across 298 social media threat incidents, based on news reports about each one. The most common response, identified in at least 176 cases, was to increase police presence at the targeted school. News reports specified that classes or the school day were canceled in at least 71 cases, while lockdowns or lockouts were implemented in at least 50 cases.[1] Figure 4.1 provides an overview of some of the response options recorded in new reports about our sample of events, as well as their frequency.

Law enforcement officers who have responded to social media–based threats against schools note that generalizations about responses are difficult to make due in part to the

FIGURE 4.1

Overview of Reported School and Local Education Agency Responses to Social Media–Based Threats, 2012–2022

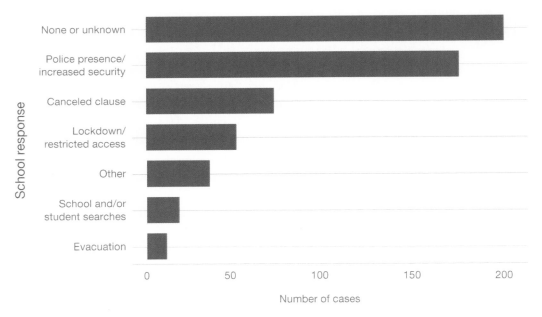

SOURCE: Features HSOAC analysis of news reports about social media threats against K–12 schools. For more information, see the discussion of the sourcing approach and methods in Chapter 1.

---

[1] These response options are not mutually exclusive, meaning that schools or local education agencies sometimes implemented more than one response following a social media–based threat, either simultaneously or sequentially. News reports indicated that a school or local education agency implemented two responses across 42 incidents in our sample; three response options were implemented in 11 cases.

unique nature of each threat and of each targeted school (Desai, 2022). One commonality is that local education agencies often have little to go with when it comes to accurately anticipating, let alone predicting, when a threat will lead to actual violence (Cornell and Maeng, 2020; Van Brunt, 2016; Amman et al., 2017). This makes choosing "the right" response action difficult, at best.

A number of state- and school district-level stakeholders who participated in our interviews referred to the I Love U Guys Foundation's Standard Response Protocol (SRP) when asked to describe how they respond to threats.[2] The protocol, which is meant to serve as a "classroom response enhancement for critical incidents," provides local education agencies and first responders with shared language and actions in an effort to promote more uniform responses across a wide range of emergencies (I Love U Guys Foundation, 2022). The main premise of the action-based protocol is that five actions are available to local education agencies during incidents. These are also the most common response actions that we read about in news reports about social media threats to schools and heard about in interviews with various K–12 school safety stakeholders:

- **Hold:** "In your Room or Area. Clear the Halls"
- **Secure:** "Get Inside, Lock Outside Doors"
- **Lockdown:** "Locks, Lights, Out of Sight"
- **Evacuate:** should be followed by a specific location
- **Shelter:** should be followed by the specific hazard and associated safety strategy.

As situations change and local education agencies and law enforcement partners gather more information about an incident or threat, these actions can be sequenced (I Love U Guys Foundation, 2022).

Despite the availability of protocols such as the I Love U Guys Foundation SRP, our interviews with school safety stakeholders across the country revealed that there is relatively little in the way of "specific and consistent guidance" around responding to threats from social media; there is also no "standard of care" dictating what an appropriate response might look like.[3] District-level emergency response protocols often vary wildly even within a state, as does the nature of intelligence about threats. This makes it nearly impossible to develop one-size-fits-all guidance.[4] What guidance does exist typically focuses on *how* to implement various response strategies rather than how to make decisions about *which one(s)* to implement.

---

[2] Representatives from state-level school safety agencies in two states, interviews with the authors, February 2023; school district representatives in two districts, interviews with the authors, January and March 2023. The I Love U Guys Foundation develops safety and family reunification programs for schools and the broader community, and also delivers trainings to improve responses to school crises.

[3] State-level school safety representative, interview with the authors, February 2023.

[4] Representatives from state-level school safety agencies in three states, interviews with the authors, January–February 2023; state-level law enforcement representative, interview with the authors, February 2023; school district representative, interview with the authors, March 2023.

In Kentucky, for example, the state's Center for School Safety provides useful information on how to implement age-appropriate lockdowns in elementary school settings, as well as how to conduct lockdown drills in a way that minimizes negative impacts on students (Kentucky Center for School Safety, undated). The state of Illinois has collected information on past investigations of social media–based threats, but beyond encouraging schools to review upcoming school events and consider lockdown strategies, most of the suggestions focus on investigations rather than response (Illinois Terrorism Task Force School Safety Working Group, 2018b).

A common concern of district-level and law enforcement stakeholders responsible for making response decisions is striking a balance between over- and under-responding.[5] Responding without overreacting is a common challenge (Burnette, Datta, Cornell, 2018; Newman, 2011; Rich and Cox, 2018).

Through our interviews, we learned that local education agency responses to social media–based threats hinge on the nature of incoming information.[6] Generally speaking, our interview participants agreed that the specificity of a threat—for example when a school or specific school building is directly named in the threatening communication—raises alarms and frequently calls for more overt or intense responses, such as full lockdowns, evacuations, or school closures.[7] As one representative from a local law enforcement agency noted, "Increasing specificity and targeting methodology suggests it's better to be safe than sorry. Put the school in lockdown and observe what happens next. If the threats continue, it's likely a more serious problem. If you never hear from [that individual] again, it will likely have been a random, swatting-like threat."[8]

At the same time, however, local education agencies commonly strive to start with the least disruptive response, based on the recommendations of their local law enforcement partners. For instance, one district-level representative told us that their initial reaction often involves temporarily adding police officers to protect the threatened schools for the day or two following a threat; this is a relatively easy response to implement and also shows to the community that the local education agency is doing something to protect students.[9] If new information adds weight to a threat, additional measures can be implemented, and the response can be scaled up.[10]

---

[5] State law enforcement representative, interview with the authors, February 2023; state-level school safety representative, interview with the authors, February 2023; school district stakeholder, interview with the authors, February 2023; local law enforcement representative, interview with the authors, February 2023.

[6] County criminal justice agency representative, interview with the authors, February 2023.

[7] School district representatives from three districts, interviews with the authors, January and February 2023; state law enforcement agency representative, interview with the authors, March 2023; local law enforcement agency representative, interview with the authors, February 2023.

[8] Local law enforcement representative, interview with the authors, February 2023.

[9] School district representative, interview with the authors, March 2023.

[10] Local law enforcement representative, interview with the authors, February 2023.

A number of school district-level stakeholders who participated in our interviews also told us that they have yet to completely close a school in response to a social media threat, preferring instead to take other steps that are less disruptive to the school day, such as implementing a hold or lockout that restricts movement into and out of the school.[11] These approaches both allow instruction to continue inside locked classrooms and grant a school more control over students' movement inside the building. Overall, they help to minimize what one local education agency representative referred to as the "drama and trauma" associated with social media–based threats.[12]

Indeed, *how* these less-disruptive responses are implemented is equally as important as choosing to implement them in the first place. Referring to decisions to increase law enforcement presence on a school campus, one interview participant highlighted that for their response strategy "*how* [law enforcement] responds matters. Part of [an effective strategy] is having schools lower the temperature of their response, but still react sufficiently. When [police] get to a school, the team includes two or three plainclothes officers. So students still only see their SRO at the school, and not the other police officers, which might concern them."[13]

Balancing Response Actions to Minimize Multiple Risks and Costs

Balancing the need to react effectively should a threat prove real while also denying hoax threateners their goal of significantly disrupting the school day makes choosing how to respond particularly difficult. Often, social media threats (and episodes of swatting) are trying to elicit an overwhelming response from the targeted school and its law enforcement partners simply to sow chaos; other times, students are trying to get out of school. When responding to a threat, the same visible police presence designed to reassure some segments of the school community (e.g., parents or staff) could be traumatizing to others (e.g., students). Carefully thinking about how to balance a response based on available information cannot only minimize disruption and trauma for the school community, but also serve as a deterrent for future threats. As one district-level stakeholder told us, "[Schools] don't want an external actor to yank [their] chain and dictate [their] response."[14] Another representative from a different district also spoke from experience: "Not responding [in the way they wanted us to] became a disincentive for kids posting these threats. They eventually realized they weren't going to get out of class."[15]

---

[11] School district representatives from four districts, interviews with the authors, February and March 2023.

[12] School district representative, interview with the authors, January 2023.

[13] Local law enforcement agency representative, interview with the authors, February 2023.

[14] School district representative, interview with the authors, January 2023.

[15] School district representative, interview with the authors, February 2023.

Drawing on the literature and our discussions with K–12 stakeholders, we assess that options for responding to anonymous social media threats differ along two key dimensions, each of which impacts the different risks and costs local education agencies seek to manage:

- **intensity of the response**—from lower intensity responses such as increased door checks to higher intensity responses involving an immediate Special Weapons and Tactics (SWAT) response to the threatened school
- **overtness of the response**—from more subtle responses such as school "lockouts" or "holds" that might not affect students or teaching at all to very overt responses such as uniformed tactical personnel responding to the threatened school.

In general, high-intensity and overt responses are the fastest and most effective response to actual threat incidents. They can, however, prove traumatizing to the school community and risk reinforcing incentives for hoax threateners who deliberately seek out highly disruptive responses. By contrast, lower intensity and less overt responses reduce both the potentially traumatic impact of response actions and the incentive to stage hoax threats; in the case of real threats, however, they may be too slow.

In considering how to respond to threats, some interviewees emphasized the value of staged responses, which help local education agencies manage the risks and costs of under- and over-response. As noted above, stakeholders described their efforts to start with less intense, less overt responses but also being prepared to move to more intense, overt actions if additional information indicated the threat was more likely to be viable. Figures 4.2 through 4.4 show how different types of responses vary in intensity and overtness and the paths that exist for scaling up responses to threats. The three figures focus on three different classes of response:

- responses involving the addition of security personnel (including law enforcement) to school grounds (Figure 4.2)
- responses focused on restricting movement within the school, as well as into and out of school buildings, including different variations of lockdowns (Figure 4.3)
- response actions aimed at keeping armed students (and others) outside the school (Figure 4.4).

Direct response by law enforcement officers, particularly tactical officers like SWAT or bomb squad personnel, represent the most overt and intense response option after a school has received a threat of violence (Figure 4.2). In swatting incidents specifically, callers purposefully seek out such responses by creating a sense of urgency around an immediate threat to life. In our interviews, both law enforcement and local education agency personnel described a number of alternative response options that were both less overt and lower in intensity. These included responses by fewer plainclothes or uniformed law enforcement officers in an effort to reduce the personnel costs of responding to individual threats, minimize the impact of response on the school community, and decrease incentives for future hoax threats.

During our interviews, one stakeholder suggested that one way to ensure preparedness in this regard was to enable quick on-scene information gathering at the targeted school (e.g., by

FIGURE 4.2

Law Enforcement or Security Personnel Response Options for Threatened Schools

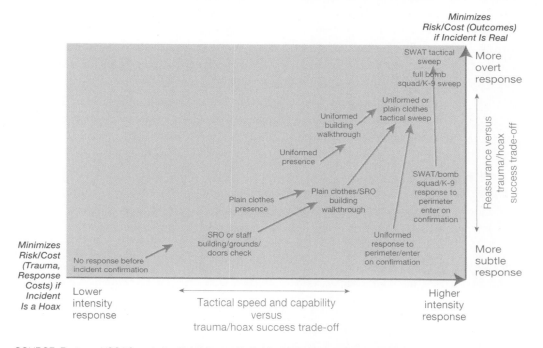

SOURCE: Features HSOAC analysis of interviews with K–12 stakeholders and law enforcement agencies.

an SRO or other designated school staff member); any relevant, up-to-date information could then be communicated back to law enforcement to minimize unnecessary responses (e.g., by quickly determining that there was not an ongoing incident at the school).[16] Other locations have dealt with a somewhat opposite dynamic: One state-level law enforcement representative noted that at times school administrators do not take law enforcement's recommendations for a low-profile response (such as posting a plainclothes officer at a school for extra security), fearing that their community will perceive the school's reaction to a threat as a nonresponse.[17]

Actions such as closing school, evacuating students,[18] and implementing a full campus lockdown requiring students to hide in protected areas are additional early response options

---

[16] State and federal law enforcement agency representatives, interviews with the authors, February 2023.

[17] State law enforcement representative, interview with the authors, February 2023.

[18] In an interview with a state law enforcement agency representative, participants noted that the practice evacuating students (which used to be the standard response to bomb threats) carries concerns for additional risk in the current environment. Specifically, if an attacker is planning a shooting incident, evacuating the school population to an outdoor location in response to a bomb threat would put students and staff in a potentially highly vulnerable position. That represents an additional risk that must be balanced in response decisionmaking (federal law enforcement agency representative, interview with the authors, March 2023). For similar concerns, see Isger (2016).

for most schools targeted by a social media–based threat (Figure 4.3). In our interviews, some local education agencies observed that they approached such options in a phased way, providing the basis for the increased response path depicted by the arrow in Figure 4.3. The first level at which a school's response might succeed in keeping a threat "out of the school" involves lockout operations, which affect only people coming into the school. Because this particular response allows for instruction to continue as normal, lockouts (or "holds") minimize any impact to students and school staff. Higher level responses included different variants of "instructional lockdowns" (where classrooms are locked and student movement is restricted), and full lockdowns where it becomes clear to individuals inside the school that measures are being taken in response to a threat.

Finally, the third category of responses we identified over the course of our interviews involves actions designed to keep weapons or armed individuals out of school buildings (Figure 4.4). These actions differ significantly depending on whether the identity of the individual making the threat is known or not (the latter being the more common situation when it comes to social media threats). When a threatener's identity is known to a school, the

FIGURE 4.3

Campus Movement Restriction and Closure Options for Threatened Schools

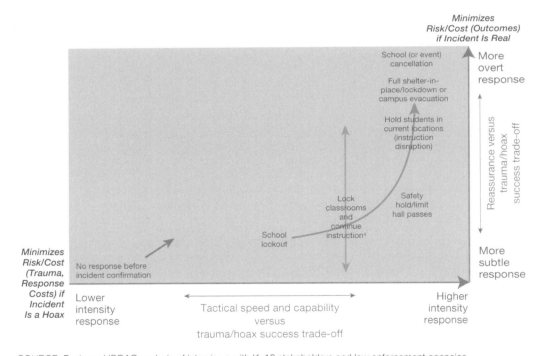

SOURCE: Features HSOAC analysis of interviews with K–12 stakeholders and law enforcement agencies.

[a] How overt or subtle just locking classrooms and continuing instruction is depends on standard practice for a specific school. For instance, in a school where teachers did not lock classrooms routinely, having them do so could be a somewhat overt action suggesting to students that something was wrong. By contrast, if locking classroom doors was an everyday practice at the school, having a teacher do so in response to a threat would have little to no effect on students.

FIGURE 4.4

Weapons Exclusion Options for Threatened Schools

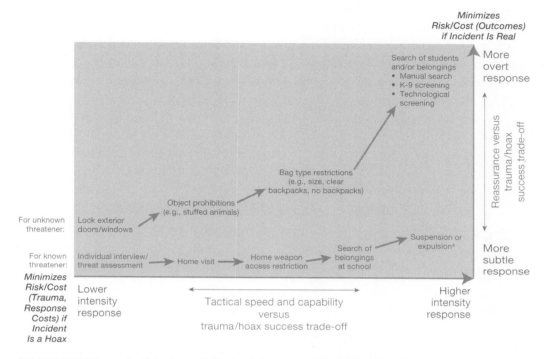

SOURCE: HSOAC analysis of interviews with K–12 stakeholders and law enforcement agencies.

[a] In addition to school discipline measures that could remove a threatening student, criminal justice action might also be taken. In the event of an identified adult threatening a school, those actions would be primary (though the adult would also likely be banned from entry to the school).

response action can be very focused—typically escalating from a threat assessment to interventions with the student or family to either limit access to weapons or prevent the student from coming to school. From the perspective of the broader school community, such interventions are not overt; usually they are individually focused and implemented in the context of law enforcement or school-based disciplinary intervention protected by student privacy laws.

When a threat is anonymous, however, interventions to detect weapons and keep them out of schools have broader effects on the entire school community. The least overt options might focus on maintaining the integrity of the school's physical perimeter, such as making sure that doors that are supposed to be locked are indeed locked. More intense and overt options might focus on searching students and their belongings. Intermediate options include restricting students from bringing specific items that could help conceal weapons (e.g., stuffed animals, certain size backpacks) or requiring them to use transparent backpacks. The most overt and intrusive option in this response category might include the deployment of teams to search belongings for weapons, including canine teams or the installation of security technology such as metal detectors. While these measures potentially provide a greater chance of excluding weapons from the school in response to a threat, some of the more visible ones—such as metal detectors—have been linked to lower perceptions of feeling safe at school in previous research (Perumean-Chaney and Sutton, 2013; Hankin, Hertz, and Simon 2011). Our interview participants also noted that certain measures such as searches can disrupt education, given the time required to search all individuals entering buildings at larger schools.[19]

Across all three response categories, local education agencies experience trade-offs; it is impossible to minimize all costs all at once. As a result, there is no "right answer" when it comes to responding to social media threats, and local expectations and concerns will necessarily shape initial responses. Nevertheless, the range of options that are available to local education agencies across the different categories of response provides some flexibility for those responsible for security planning and those who seek to balance the different concerns created by social media threats of violence.

Additional Challenges in Response Decisionmaking and Implementation

Beyond the difficulty of balancing how to respond to social media threats, our interviewees also flagged two other issues: (1) the effect of the timing of threats on decisionmaking and viable response options; and (2) how repeated threats and intense responses can create complacency in the school community.

The specific timing of social media–based threats can complicate response. A threat received outside of school hours, for instance, over the weekend, gives local education agencies and their law enforcement partners more time to investigate without needing to make changes to the school day. They might respond proactively by conducting searches of a school overnight, and screen students and staff for weapons as they arrive the next morning.[20] By contrast, threats that come in when students and staff are in school necessitate a more immediate response that could affect teaching and learning. As one district-level stakeholder explained, "If [threats come in] during the day when kids are in school, there isn't time. We have to alert the police department, office administrators, and make a plan from there."[21] Experts we consulted also emphasized that the value of "extending the timeline" for responding to a threat further reinforces the need to build a positive school climate that supports bystander reporting: The prompt reporting of social media threats by students, parents, or staff will give school officials and law enforcement more time to implement a balanced response (Moore et al., 2022).

---

[19] School district representatives from two districts, interviews with the authors, February and March 2023.

[20] State law enforcement representative, interview with the authors, February 2023; state-level school safety representative, interview with the authors, February 2023; school district representatives from two districts, interviews with the authors, February and March 2023.

[21] School district representative, interview with the authors, February 2023.

An associated challenge relates to avoiding complacency. School safety experts and our interview participants have noted that repeated use of lockdowns as an initial blanket response to commonplace social media threats can become too repetitive and reduce staff readiness in the face of a real-life incident (Blad, 2022).[22] For instance, school safety representatives in state-level agencies expressed concern that school administrators are becoming desensitized to repeated threats and automatically dismissing them as hoaxes, rather than treating them as potentially real events.[23]

Coordinating Response Across Local Education Agency and Law Enforcement Personnel

As the preceding section suggests, coordinating with law enforcement is critical to responding to social media–based threats against K–12 schools. Yet, despite both law enforcement and local education agencies' acknowledgement of the importance of doing so, many face challenges in this area. Often, coordination is difficult simply due to siloed environments. In our interviews, district- and state-level stakeholders highlighted the need for better training about social media threats for both school staff and law enforcement personnel.[24] Some local education agency-level stakeholders stressed the need for more school-specific response training for police, specifically training to enhance their understanding of response protocols in place at individual schools in their communities.[25] School safety personnel also reported that improving law enforcement agencies' understanding of designated areas for school evacuations, as well as the practical implications of specific response terminology (such as "hold" versus "secure"), is especially urgent.[26] As one state-level school safety representative noted, "If law enforcement doesn't know about the option to put a school in a safety hold, then they won't call it."[27] Local education agency leaders shared similar opinions: "There is a need for systematic training for law enforcement that gives guidance on district and school response plans and protocols. It's hard to train; there is lots of variability [across districts]."[28]

---

[22] Representatives from state-level school safety agencies in two states, interviews with the authors, March 2023; school district representative, interview with the authors, March 2023.

[23] State-level school safety representative, interview with the authors, March 2023.

[24] School district representatives in two districts, interviews with the authors, February 2023; state-level school safety representative, interview with the authors, February 2023.

[25] School district representative, interview with the authors, February 2023.

[26] State-level school safety representative, interview with the authors, February 2023; state law enforcement agency representative, interview with the authors, February 2023.

[27] State-level school safety representative, interview with the authors, February 2023.

[28] School district representative, interview with the authors, February 2023.

Coordination across different levels of law enforcement—for example between school-based police and local, state, and federal law enforcement—has also proved challenging. The challenges can also differ from location to location. For example, one local law enforcement agency experienced a lag when reaching out to federal-level law enforcement resources such as the Joint Terrorism Task Forces when investigating a threat, while a similar representative in another part of the country talked about a very effective working relationship with the group in their geographical area.[29] Representatives from state-level law enforcement agencies also explained that "one of the hardest things to navigate [after a threat] is who has control of information and communication. It can be difficult to understand who is running command and control, whether it's local law enforcement or the school security officer."[30] These challenges are not unique to responses to social media threats against schools; in fact, critical incident and after-action reviews of numerous mass attacks point to communication and coordination challenges during multi-agency responses and highlight the important role that precoordination, joint training exercises, and other initiatives can play in avoiding complications during responses to emergencies (see, e.g., Straub et al., 2019; National Police Foundation, 2018).

A number of local education agencies that have been the target of social media–based and other threats face entirely different challenges, largely as a result of calls to reduce police presence in schools after high-profile incidents of police violence in recent years (Cowan, Hubler, and Taylor, 2021). We heard this from large urban districts that made cuts to their school police forces,[31] with one local education agency representative telling us that "the removal of police officers from schools . . . has had a taxing impact because we now don't have the right officers or enough of them to respond to threats."[32] That said, record levels of gun violence in K–12 schools in 2022 and rising numbers of threats of violence have caused some major urban districts to reverse their decisions to eliminate school-based police (Arango, 2023).

Our search for guidance about how to coordinate local education agency and law enforcement responses to social media–based threats revealed a lack of resources in this area. What we did identify focused on related types of threats (such as bomb threats and swatting threats), which speak only indirectly to social media–based threats. For instance, a resource from the National Emergency Number Association (NENA) that is focused on swatting outlines steps for advance coordination with emergency responders, highlighting the importance of understanding the standard operating procedures of various agencies across different types of emergencies, as well as their unique roles and responsibilities; doing so can help streamline response in otherwise complex environments (NENA, undated). Guidance from the Department of Justice Community Oriented Policing Services also emphasizes the importance of

---

[29] Local law enforcement agency representative, interview with the authors, February 2023.

[30] State law enforcement agency representative, interview with the authors, February 2023.

[31] School district representatives in two districts, interviews with the authors, January and February 2023; local law enforcement agency representative, interview with the authors, February 2023.

[32] School district representative, interview with the authors, February 2023.

establishing a strong working relationship between local law enforcement and local education agencies (Newman, 2011).

Indeed, representatives from local education agencies across the country stressed the importance of close, collaborative relationships with their local law enforcement partners when deciding on how to respond to social media threats; many explained that they rely first and foremost on these partners' recommendations before implementing a hold, lockdown, or other response.[33] Deep partnerships that have been built up between local education agencies and law enforcement over time help to develop trust and make it possible for collaboration during threat incidents to happen freely and openly; everyday engagement between the two entities, especially in between incidents, helps to sustain these trusting relationships.[34] A school's SRO or school police department in particular can serve as the critical liaison between the school and local law enforcement agencies, which often have unique capabilities to help local education agencies address a threat and respond appropriately.[35]

Interview participants highlighted many of these capabilities in our discussions about responding to social media–based threats. Law enforcement personnel can frequently take response actions that go beyond what school personnel can do in a threat situation, such as home visits to ensure that a threatening individual does not have access to a weapon.[36] But they can also take key actions that would allow local education agencies to minimize the visibility of a response to a threat, depending on when the threat comes in. As noted previously, police can conduct precursor checks at the targeted school with canine teams or other explosives detection technologies, or they can deploy weapon abatement teams to screen students and staff upon arrival on the day of a named threat.[37]

The resources that certain law enforcement agencies such as state intelligence fusion centers provide can also help local education agencies respond more appropriately to threats by sharing information across various stakeholders to ascertain the origin of a threat, determining whether other schools or districts (including districts in other states) have received similar threats, and specifying what others are doing to respond (REMS TA Center, undated).[38] These centers can also engage federal law enforcement resources as necessary and gain access to additional intelligence that can help local education agencies make better informed response

---

[33] School district representatives in five districts, interviews with the authors, January and February 2023.

[34] School district representative, interview with the authors, February 2023; federal law enforcement agency representative, interview with the authors, March 2023.

[35] School district representative, interview with the authors, January 2023.

[36] School district representatives, interview with the authors, January and February 2023.

[37] State law enforcement agency representative, interview with the authors, February 2023; school district representative, interview with the authors, March 2023.

[38] An intelligence fusion center is established by state and local governments to coordinate the gathering, sharing, analysis, and dissemination of information related to terrorism, public safety, and criminal justice activity (REMS TA Center, undated; Abamu, 2018).

decisions.[39] While most activities conducted by intelligence fusion centers take place outside of the public domain (Abamu, 2018), the process of information sharing—across local, state, and in some cases federal law enforcement partners—has been critical to helping many local education agencies across the country respond to social media threats.[40]

Communicating with Families During and After a Threat

Communication with families is critical as local education agencies respond to social media–based and other types of threats. Perhaps most unique to this particular type of threat is the speed at which it can spread across various social media platforms once it has been posted and the associated misinformation and rumors that also begin to proliferate along with it. Whereas guidance around communication in the event of threats used to be "release complete information only when you have it," today's social media environment incentivizes local education agencies to release information to their community "as quickly as possible" and to do so in a way that guards against panic.[41] Indeed, stakeholders from local education agencies told us that "rumors and exaggeration about a threat are especially difficult to control,"[42] and the media also sometimes add pressure on local education agencies and law enforcement to provide more information, faster.[43] But releasing information that is "not vetted and too raw" often only worsens the situation.[44] Furthermore, the ubiquity of smartphones and similar mobile devices among today's youth also means that parents and others outside an affected school receive unofficial information about a threat and the associated response in piecemeal fashion, often from panicked children. As one interviewee noted, "If [local education agencies] don't communicate anything, everyone's cell phone will be blowing up with stories and speculation."[45] In other words, it is incumbent, if extremely challenging, on local education agencies to send a message out to their community that is at once timely, accurate, does not compromise any ongoing investigation, and demonstrates that the school and its law enforcement partners are taking active steps to control the situation and keep the community safe.

What are local education agencies doing in response to some of these challenges? In our research, we found that sharing basic threat and emergency response plans regularly with families—outside of threat events—can help better prepare the school community for

---

[39] State-level school safety representative, interview with the authors, January 2023; state and federal law enforcement agency representatives, interviews with the authors, February 2023.

[40] State law enforcement agency representative, interview with the authors, March 2023; school district representative, interview with the authors, March 2023.

[41] School district representative, interview with the authors, February 2023.

[42] School district representative, interview with the authors, March 2023.

[43] State-level school safety representative, interview with the authors, February 2023.

[44] School district representative, interview with the authors, February 2023.

[45] School district representative, interview with the authors, March 2023.

actual emergencies and alleviate some of the panic that threat situations induce (Blad, 2022). Indeed, the National Association of School Resource Officers (NASRO, 2022) has highlighted that a surge in parents arriving to pick up their children at school during a potential incident has been a significant interruption to law enforcement and other response efforts. Response actions can flow more smoothly and some of the traumatic impacts of threats can be lessened when parents and other community members are aware of protocols that will be followed during a threat event. Transparency about how threat responses are implemented can also reduce pressure on school leaders or law enforcement during and after a threat—for example, from understandably concerned parents or decisionmakers who are more comfortable erring on the side of over- rather than under-reacting—to take more overt or intense actions that could be more traumatic for students.

While local education agencies should not be expected to share exact details of their response protocols for security reasons, communicating what a response would look like in the face of active threat situations can help enhance preparedness across the student and staff population, as well as among families (Perez, 2022; Witsil, 2022). Representatives from local education agencies with whom we spoke also found that regularly communicating with families during active shooter and other types of drills has similar benefits.[46] Those working in the school safety field regularly offer communication tips to districts, such as encouraging districts to take steps to provide their communities with adequate details about the type of threat, why a specific precaution is in place, and what safeguards the school is taking with students who are present (Blad, 2022; Illinois Terrorism Task Force School Safety Working Group, 2018a). Experts note that consistency in messaging is key: School administrators, local law enforcement, and any other responding agencies should work to disseminate the same message about a specific threat situation in an effort to avoid the spread of misinformation (Illinois Terrorism Task Force School Safety Working Group, 2018a).

Our interviews with K–12 stakeholders provided some examples of how local education agencies across the country implement these and other recommendations to improve communications during threat situations. For instance, a number of representatives from state-level school safety offices told us that messages from local education agencies in their states during social media threat situations include an acknowledgement that a threat has been received; a description of basic actions taken by the school and law enforcement to respond to the threat; confirmation that students and staff are safe; and any directions to reunification or early pickup locations.[47] Community messages about threat situations can also include information about whom to contact with questions, as well as reminders about expectations for social media behavior and the importance of reporting.[48] Some state-level school safety agencies provide assistance in this area, including offering training on how to converse with

---

[46] State-level school safety representative, interview with the authors, February 2023.

[47] Representatives from state-level school safety agencies in four states, interviews with the authors, February and March 2023.

[48] State-level school safety representative, interview with the authors, February 2023.

families during an incident, preparing template response statements as part of emergency planning efforts, and making written communications more accessible to a wider variety of audiences.[49] As one local education agency representative explained, "It's really important to have schools acknowledging the threat was received and describe any ongoing actions. [Schools] need the transparency to build the trust and controlling the message is necessary. If the schools don't tell the story, someone else will."[50]

Our interview participants also emphasized the importance of using multiple modes of communication available to reach out to families, including email, phone calls, the school website, and various social media platforms. One district reported plans to use live text messaging in their mass communication plan, which is often a faster way to contact families than phone calls.[51] To some extent, such steps can also help address challenges related to outdated parent and caretaker contact information, as well as concerns over limited access to certain forms of communication, such as email, in some communities.[52]

Addressing the Impacts of Response

Addressing every potential negative impact is a serious challenge for schools and their law enforcement partners (Rich and Cox, 2018; Perez, 2022; Kentucky Center for School Safety, undated; Yechivi, 2022). Often, local education agencies need to make mental health resources and other forms of assistance available to students and staff in the wake of a threat, even if it does not result in an active incident (Rich and Cox, 2018; Perez, 2022). School counselors, social workers, and school psychologists have been critical resources for local education agencies and their broader communities in this regard.[53] More preparation—repeated practice and drills over what to do in the event of an incident such as an active shooter—can also help local education agencies and their communities better cope with the impacts of threats, provided that they are implemented in age and developmentally appropriate ways and that students, teachers, and other school staff are given opportunities to share their reactions to the drill once it is over (Yechivi, 2022; Schildkraut and Nickerson, 2022; Kentucky Center for School Safety, undated). Indeed, even drills can be a source of trauma for many school-aged children, especially those who have already experienced trauma in the past (Mascia, 2022). Organizations such as NASRO and the National Association of School Psychologists (NASP) have developed best practices guidance in this area to support local education agencies in

---

[49] Representatives from state-level school safety agencies in five states, interviews with the authors, February and March 2023.

[50] School district representative, interview with the authors, March 2023.

[51] School district representative, interview with the authors, February 2023.

[52] State-level school safety representative, interview with the authors, February 2023; school district representative, interview with the authors, March 2023.

[53] Local law enforcement agency representative, interview with the authors, February 2023.

planning drills in a way that minimizes both impacts on student and staff mental and physical well-being and disruptions to teaching and learning (NASP and NASRO, 2021).

Preventing Future Threats

In the aftermath of dealing with threats, many local education agencies have redirected their prevention efforts to also take into account social media activity. Many, for instance, have invested in software to detect threats in student writing and social media use (Social Sentinel, Go Guardian, and Gaggle are some common examples of such software) (O'Leary, 2022). Schools have also found it helpful to communicate clear social media guidelines to students and families, informing them about what could constitute a threat and reinforcing the importance of reporting by instructing them on what do to when they see a threat online (i.e., report it, don't repost it) (School Safety Grant, 2020; Perez, 2022). Our interview participants also described their own outreach and training efforts regarding appropriate social media behavior, which focus in part on recognizing threats, reporting them, and the damage that threatening communications can cause.[54] In many areas, however, stakeholders still view this as a critical area for improvement.[55] One district-level representative, for instance, told us that "most kids don't realize the damage that these sorts of [threatening] communications can cause. There is more that can be done in this area."[56]

Outreach and training for parents are especially important, given that most social media activity takes place at home. In this regard, our interview participants underscored the need to raise parent awareness of social media activity in particular and provide parents with tools to help them recognize potential threats and report them via appropriate channels.[57] While parents may be hesitant to monitor their children's social media accounts for fear of invading their privacy, "[they] need to know what kids are doing. When parents are more involved and checking in, it's helpful [to schools seeking to address threats]."[58]

Outreach and training in this area take many forms, ranging from all-school assemblies about social media behavior, posting information about social media and electronic device usage on local education agency websites, and hosting parent classes on internet safety.[59] Some local education agencies have also taken to disseminating their own social media

---

[54] School district representatives in two districts, interviews with the authors, January and February 2023; representatives from state-level school safety agencies in three states, interviews with the authors, January and February 2023.

[55] School district representatives in two districts, interviews with the authors, February and March 2023; state-level school safety agency representative, February 2023.

[56] School district representative, interview with the authors, February 2023.

[57] School district representatives in three districts, interviews with the authors, January–March 2023.

[58] School district representative, interview with the authors, January 2023.

[59] School district representatives in two districts, interviews with the authors, February and March 2023.

posts about myriad social media–based "challenges" that often prompt an onslaught of hoax threats, confirming to their communities that they are aware of the trend and asking members to not contribute to its spread.[60] The Texas School Safety Center has also published a resource with Safer Schools Together that introduces major social media platforms, games, and relevant trends to familiarize school personnel with diverse platforms as part of their preparedness efforts (Safer Schools Together, Texas School Safety Center, and International Center for Digital Threat Assessment, 2022).

Notably, a number of interviewees connected their efforts to thwart social media threats to ongoing suicide prevention efforts; in many cases, it seems as though social media–based and other threats made by students are cries for help.[61] Recent mass shootings inside and outside of school environments show that expressions of suicidal intent often precede acts of targeted violence (Stephenson, 2023; Williams, Bogel-Burroughs, and Arango, 2023). Studies also show that mass shooters have many traits in common with individuals who die by suicide compared with other members of the general population (Lankford, Silver, and Cox, 2021). As one law enforcement officer who works with local education agencies in the aftermath of threats noted, "In many respects, [preventing future threats] is a matter of having counselors, teachers, parents, and others understand that 'earlier is better.' So many of these [threats] are cries for help as opposed to real intent to do harm. When we can better identify needs for help early on, we'll preempt the threats. Early support and intervention may mean a kid doesn't go down a path where they up doing this kind of stuff."[62]

Finally, our interviews revealed that some local education agencies and their law enforcement partners hope that communicating the potential consequences faced by those identified as making threats can help to deter students from doing something that could have long-term consequences for themselves and others. A number of states around the country have already passed laws making threats against schools a criminal offense (see, e.g., Feldman, 2018; Blizzard and Richter, 2022; Smith, 2018; Ainsworth, 2022), as has the federal government (FBI, 2018). The most common refrain from our stakeholders about this topic was the potential deterrence power of visible consequences: "Kids do see what happens—they see the example [of someone being arrested or suspended] and they don't want to be a part of it."[63] Not knowing that there are consequences, on the other hand, may suggest to students that they can continue to get away with making threats that will get them out of school for a day.[64]

Nevertheless, some stakeholders also described that there are limits to how much schools and law enforcement agencies can publicize consequences, given privacy laws that protect

---

[60] State-level school safety agency representative, interview with the authors, February 2023.

[61] School district representative, interview with the authors, January 2023.

[62] Local law enforcement agency representative, interview with the authors, February 2023.

[63] School district representative, interview with the authors, March 2023.

[64] State-level school safety agency representative, interview with the authors, February 2023.

the identity of juveniles charged with crimes or facing school disciplinary measures. But they may not need to do so; media coverage about threat incidents—for example, an article detailing that a responsible party was identified, subsequently arrested, and charged—can help to deter most from committing a similar offense.[65] Moreover, "Kids talk; they put two and two together, and they can usually figure out who it was who made the threat and what happened to them."[66]

Despite the potential deterrent effect of consequences at the individual level, even this decision is a difficult one to make for local education agencies. In other words, there is another balanced decision that local education agencies must make in response to social media threats, this time about determining consequences for individuals (usually students) who make them. Threat-assessment teams and ensuing interventions/risk management strategies often seek to minimize severe punishment such as expulsion or involving the criminal justice system, especially for what is ultimately attention-seeking behavior. In discussions during this study, experts emphasized that "threats are made by students who have problems that they can't solve," and so it is more important to respond to those root causes than to focus on punishment in hopes of deterring others. Such a strategy would also risk the positive school climate needed to promote student willingness to report threats, with broader consequences for safety. That said, when a threat disrupts and traumatizes entire schools—and sometimes all schools in a district as well as schools in neighboring local education agencies—making clear to students that there are higher-level consequences, ones that often must involve the criminal justice system, becomes increasingly critical to help to deter future threats and avoid mass disruptions.

Conclusion

Informed, balanced responses to social media–based threats against K–12 schools help minimize disruption to the school community while still keeping its members safe. News of a threat need not call for emergency closures and the panic and widespread media attention that these often incite. Instead, local education agencies should work with their law enforcement partners to determine how a less disruptive yet still robust response can address the dual goals of getting on with the school day and ensuring safety. Responses can always be scaled up if new intelligence adds weight to a threat. Most importantly, stakeholders who participated in our interviews emphasized the importance of educating schools "to have a unified approach and follow a specific protocol."[67] This is also what the I Love You Guys Foundation strives to do with its SRP (I Love You Guys Foundation, 2022). In doing so, there are likely to be fewer knee-jerk reactions and less stress. As one district-level stakeholder with

---

[65] School district representative, interview with the authors, March 2023.

[66] School district representative, interview with the authors, March 2023.

[67] County criminal justice agency representative, interview with the authors, February 2023.

extensive experience in this area emphasized, "[Local education agencies] have to train leaders to make clear decisions in ambiguous situations. We have tried to balance the yin and yang of physical safety and emotional/psychological safety. It isn't just this versus that. . . . [Responding to threats] is essentially a symbiosis: You have to design your physical [safety] protocol to avoid unnecessarily lurching into high gear all the time."[68]

Ultimately, responding to social media–based and other types of threats to K–12 schools can be viewed as a triangle: "The base is the school system. They have the oversight, the connectivity with the kids. Another side is the counseling staff, and the other staff is the SRO or other school-based law enforcement. When you look at appropriate intervention, it requires all three."[69] Trusting partnerships between local education agencies and local law enforcement agencies as well as other community partners are key to enabling measured responses. As one of our interview participants succinctly explained, "The first step [in ensuring preparedness] is to identify key partners. Local law enforcement, fusion centers, and other agencies are key. These partners bring additional resources [to schools]. Schools need to bring these people together and be on the same page as them. There can't be silos."[70]

---

[68] School district representative, interview with the authors, January 2023.

[69] Local law enforcement agency representative, interview with the authors, February 2023.

[70] County criminal justice agency representative, interview with the authors, February 2023.

CHAPTER 5

Conclusions and Implications for Stakeholders Across the K–12 Community

Dealing with threats posted on social media—and similar threats such as swatting—is a relatively new and growing challenge for local education agencies across the country. In the context of a high-threat landscape, broad exposure to and accessibility of firearms among parts of the school age population, and persistent levels of school violence, assessing whether a posted threat is real or a hoax involves high stakes. While school officials often told us they had to treat every threat as real until they could determine otherwise, even that approach has substantial challenges: intense and overt responses to repeated threats traumatize students and school staff, disrupt the educational process, and—because mass disruption is often the goal of individuals making the threats—reinforce the incentives for more threats in the future. Schools across the country are beginning to refine their strategies to protect their communities from both the risk of violence and the costs and risks associated with different responses to threats. This has not been easy. In the words of one of our interviewees,

> "The whole process can seem really intimidating. But it's really all common sense. Doing something is always better than doing nothing. You have to get past the intimidation factor. Keep your eyes and ears open and share information with key partners. Sitting in a room together with partners is so critical, to understand what each one can offer."[1]

Just as collaboration between schools and their larger communities—public safety agencies, other local organizations, as well as school staff, students, and parents—is critical to addressing other challenges, it can also help address threats in ways that balance the many concerns and risks local education agencies must manage every day.

Based on our interviews with K–12 stakeholders, analyses of news reports about social media threats, and a review of relevant literature and guidance, we learned the following:

- **Investigating social media threats—particularly anonymous ones—needs to be a multidisciplinary effort.** School personnel are not and should not need to become investigators; they should be able to rely on law enforcement and other specialist partners (e.g., psychologists) with specific capabilities to assess the urgency of a threat. In

---

[1] Representative from county criminal justice organization, interview with the authors, March 2023.

interviews, numerous school representatives emphasized the importance of their relationships with local law enforcement—including, but not limited to, SROs located in the school—when their school is the target of a threat. Our interviews also highlighted that school leaders with close connections to police utilize those connections in different ways. In some cases, interviewees from local education agencies indicated they deferred almost entirely to police when it came to assessing the viability of social media threats and also in making decisions about how to respond to these threats. In other cases, local education agencies drew on the investigative and other expertise of law enforcement but restricted decisions about how to respond to school administrators and other relevant district staff. In nearly all of our interviews, however, various stakeholders cited access to different expertise and collaboration between public safety agencies and local education agencies as important when making difficult and potentially high-stakes decisions. Sharing responsibility is critical, and agencies involved in a response should establish clear command and control protocols early on in the process.

- **Local education agency approaches to navigating social media threats need to balance risks of both under- and over-response and integrate options for escalation as new information about a threat comes in.** When responding to a threat, schools must balance the risk that a threat might be credible with the trauma and disruption that repeated responses to hoax threats induce. The more that local education agencies are able to consider and achieve that balance during school security planning, the more deliberately and effectively they will be in their response to such threats. Less overt response strategies that start at lower intensity but can be scaled up rapidly as more information about a threat becomes available are one way to strike that balance. Establishing a strong reporting culture in which students, parents, and others immediately report threats when they see them can also give decisionmakers more time to make critical response decisions.

  Another strategy for facilitating response to anonymous threats while managing trauma to students could be to integrate certain response actions—such as soft lockdowns or the presence of uniformed law enforcement officers—into more commonplace school routines or as a response to other events. For example, implementing soft lockdowns when emergency medical services or others are called to respond to a nonviolent incident at school helps to weaken the connection between that specific response measure and the risk of violence, potentially reducing the fear that students and staff feel when they see a police officer. Habituation strategies could begin to make more overt types of response less traumatizing, provided that they are implemented in ways that are appropriate in terms of age, development, and other considerations.

- **Local education agencies nationwide would likely benefit from consensus practices or an established "standard of care" for addressing social media and other anonymous threats of violence.** The potential for litigation resulting from either over- or under-responding to threats suggests the need to develop a "standard of care" for responding to threats at the national, state, or local level. Standards would be valuable for guiding decisions and supporting local school decisionmakers in (1) assessing the viability of threats; (2) identifying pathways for balancing response and escalating responses to threats based on new information; (3) coming to agreement on common vocabulary for response options that would be used by both schools and law enforcement (e.g., "secure hold"); and (4) communicating with families and the broader community during a threat response.

Some school districts across the country have already developed some of their own approaches for assessing the validity of threats, based on factors that are important to their local contexts. Differences in local needs and risk tolerance will mean that approaches will likely have to be customized to particular school districts. However, practices being developed by leading districts could be vetted by expert panels that include representation from law enforcement agencies, mental health providers, and other stakeholders to provide a starting point for developing consensus approaches.

- **Local education agencies and their law enforcement partners need new approaches for detecting and deterring social media threats.** Our interviewees emphasized that the significant impact of even hoax threats on school communities points to the need to prioritize strategies to preemptively detect threats and also deter individuals from making them. Across a number of interviews with both local education agency and law enforcement representatives, we heard about the need for real and substantial consequences for individuals who make threats, including legal consequences. In some cases—such as, for example, individuals sending hoax threats to U.S. schools from abroad—proposals to make the consequences of threat-making as severe as possible are not problematic. However, when it comes to identifying consequences for students who threaten their own or other schools, identifying the best response exposes tensions for both schools and law enforcement. One goal of K–12 threat assessment efforts and any ensuing intervention and risk mitigation strategies is to respond in a way that changes behavior without—if possible—imposing potentially lifelong consequences for poor decisions made as a youth. However, when social media threats—even attention-seeking hoaxes or cries for help—traumatize large numbers of people and impose significant costs on local education agencies and law enforcement, interviewees called into question whether achieving that goal is always possible. Thus, efforts may be best directed to educating students, parents, and others at the beginning of each school year about potential consequences—including legal consequences—of making threats against schools, even if these are intended as jokes.

If schools choose to use tools to detect threats in student writing (including on social media), these tools need to be improved to be more accurate, limit bias, and limit privacy and civil liberties concerns. Currently, schools assess that existing services such as Gaggle, Go Guardian, and Social Sentinel are largely ineffective, place a significant burden on school staff given the large number of false threats they flag, and also pose significant privacy concerns. While advances in technology may make these tools more effective over time, their current level of capability raises questions about their broad use to identify new threats (versus being used in a focused way as part of online components of investigations of already reported threats). If schools do select to use these services, administrators should make clear to their communities what service they are using, what the service monitors for, and the purpose for its use. They should also be vigilant in attending to any ways that such tools could introduce biases and flag threats in ways that might disproportionately affect some student populations (Schwartz et al., 2022).

- **Future research should focus on improving the options available to local education agencies and public safety agencies dealing with online threats.** Though the insights from our interviewees provide a view into how schools are currently dealing with social media threats, our work also emphasizes the need for continued efforts to improve on today's promising practices. Collecting data on which responses minimize the disruptive and traumatic effect of anonymous threats could ease decisionmaking burdens for school officials. Additional studies of which indicators have the greatest value in distinguishing real from hoax threats (and how those indicators shift as threateners change their behavior) could also help schools and police better navigate the issue. Future research might leverage data from local education agencies that use online monitoring software to identify threatening language to improve the use of such software and also reduce the burden on school staff to resolve numerous alerts. Finally, efforts can also focus on better integrating principles for assessing anonymous threats specifically into commonly employed threat-assessment guidelines, such as those developed by USSS's NTAC. Continued attention to these and other issues is critical to understanding how the threat landscape is changing, how individuals are turning to new technologies to threaten K–12 schools, and what schools can do to better assess and respond to threats.

Interview Protocol

1. BACKGROUND QUESTIONS
    We would like to begin by asking some general questions about your professional background in school safety/school administration/law enforcement.
    a. Could you please describe the amount and kind of experience you have had in [relevant sector]?
    b. To what extent has this experience pertained to school safety in particular?
    c. To what extent has this experience pertained to assessing threats and developing responses to threats?

2. TRENDS IN THREATS AGAINST K–12 SCHOOLS
    a. What types of trends have you observed in your school/community when it comes to threats against schools? If possible, please describe:
        i.   The types and severity of threats
        ii.   How threats are made (e.g., via social media, in person, through vandalism)
        iii. Quantity or frequency of threats
        iv.   Who is making threats; anonymity of threats
        v.   How these threats typically come to your attention.
    b. How have threats made against your school/community impacted your school/community?

3. APPROACHES TO ASSESSING CREDIBILITY OF THREATS
    a. What steps or processes do you apply to assess the credibility of anonymous threats?
        i.   Are there specific indicators that you look for to assess the credibility of threats?
        ii.   Who at your school and outside organizations is involved in this process?
    b. What types of additional resources (guides, toolkits, etc.) are available to help you assess the credibility of threats?
    c. What challenges do you face when assessing the credibility of threats?

4. APPROACHES TO RESPONDING TO ANONYMOUS THREATS
    a. What steps do you take to respond to anonymous threats?
        i.   Can you provide some examples of past responses?
        ii. Is the response to social media–based threats typically the same across threats, or have some threats received more/less intense responses than others? Why do you think that is?
    b. How do you communicate with families and the broader community after a school has received a threat?
    c. What guidance do you refer to in designing your response to threats?
    d. What challenges do you face when responding to anonymous threats?
    e. What resources or knowledge do you wish you had to improve response to anonymous threats?

5. Are there any steps that your [school/district] is taking to improve capabilities to identify threats on social media preemptively?
    a. If yes:
        i.   Do you find these steps helpful for identifying threats? Why/why not?
        ii. What challenges have you encountered in implementing these steps?
    b. If no:
        i.   Can you share some of the reasons why you are not taking any such steps?
    c. What resources or other forms of support do you wish you had in this area?

6. CONCLUDING QUESTIONS
    As we wrap up, we would like to ask
    a. Is there anything else we did not cover that we should consider?
    b. Are there any other individuals or organizations you feel we should speak to who have good visibility on these issues and can provide valuable insight for our study? Can you provide their contact information?
    c. Is there any additional documentation you could share with us that you think would be relevant to our study?

Abbreviations

CCD	Common Core Data
CISA	Cybersecurity and Infrastructure Security Agency
DHS	U.S. Department of Homeland Security
FBI	Federal Bureau of Investigation
HSOAC	Homeland Security Operational Analysis Center
IP	internet protocol
K–12	kindergarten through 12th grade
NASP	National Association of School Psychologists
NASRO	National Association of School Resource Officers
NCES	National Center for Education Statistics
NGO	nongovernmental organization
NTAC	National Threat Assessment Center
SRO	school resource officer
SRP	Standard Response Protocol
SSD	School Shooting Database
SWAT	Special Weapons and Tactics
TA	threat assessment
USSS	U.S. Secret Service
VoIP	voice over internet protocol

References

Abamu, Jenny, "Secret 'Fusion Centers' and the Search for the Next School Shooter," Edsurge, July 11, 2018.

Ainsworth, Amber, "What Is the Punishment for Making a School Threat in Michigan? AG Nessel explains potential consequences," FOX2 Detroit, November 17, 2022.

Amman, M., M. Bowlin, L. Buckles, K. C. Burton, K. F. Brunell, K. A. Gibson, and C. J. Robins, *Making Prevention a Reality: Identifying, Assessing, and Managing the Threat of Targeted Attacks*, U.S. Department of Justice, 2017.

Arango, Tim, "Schools Bring Back Police to Campuses, Reversing Racial Justice Decisions," *New York Times*, June 27, 2023.

Ashworth, Mack, "Dangerous TikTok 'School Shooting Challenge' Causes False Active Shooter Reports," Yahoo Life, March 30, 2023.

Blad, Evie, "'Swatting' Hoaxes Disrupt Schools Across the Country: What Educators Need to Know," *EdWeek*, September 21, 2022.

Blizzard, Nick, and Ed Richter, "School Threats on Rise: What's Behind It and What's Being Done," *Dayton Daily News*, November 13, 2022.

Burnette, Anna Grace, Pooja Datta, and Dewey Cornell, "The Distinction Between Transient And Substantive Student Threats," *Journal of Threat Assessment and Management*, Vol. 5, No. 1, 2018.

Burnette, Anna Grace, Timothy Konold, and Dewey Cornell, "Grade-Level Distinctions in Student Threats of Violence," *Journal of School Violence*, Vol. 19, No. 3, 2020.

Case, Angela, "Swatting Calls Came into Colorado Schools in Alphabetical Order," 9News, February 22, 2023.

Chabria, Anita, "Column: A School Threat: Do You Send Your Child or Keep Them Home?" *Los Angeles Times*, February 16, 2023.

CISA—*See* Cybersecurity and Infrastructure Security Agency.

CISA and NTAC—*See* Cybersecurity and Infrastructure Security Agency and National Threat Assessment Center.

Consortium for School Networking and National School Public Relations Association, *Schools and Social Media: A Survey of Association Members*, May–June 2022.

Cornell, Dewey G., "Guidelines for Responding to Student Threats of Violence," *Journal of Educational Administration*, Vol. 41, No. 6, 2003.

Cornell, Dewey G., and Jennifer Maeng, *Student Threat Assessment as a Safe and Supportive Prevention Strategy: Final Technical Report*, Curry School of Education, University of Virginia, 2020.

CoSN and NSPRA—*See* Consortium for School Networking and National School Public Relations Association.

Cowan, Jill, Shawn Hubler, and Kate Taylor, "Protestors Urged Defunding the Police: Schools in Big Cities Are Doing It," *New York Times*, March 8, 2021.

Cowan, Rebecca G., P. J. Tedeschi, Michael Corbin, and Rebekah Cole, "A Mixed-Methods Analysis of Averted Mass Violence in Schools: Implications for Professional School Counselors," *Psychology in the Schools*, Vol. 59, No. 4, 2022.

Cox, Joseph, "A Computer Generated Swatting Service Is Causing Havoc Across America," *Vice,* April 13, 2023.

Cybersecurity and Infrastructure Security Agency, "School Security Assessment Tool (SSAT)," webpage, undated.

Cybersecurity and Infrastructure Security Agency, *K–12 School Security Guide*, 3rd ed., 2022.

Cybersecurity and Infrastructure Security Agency and National Threat Assessment Center, *Improving School Safety Through Bystander Reporting: A Toolkit for Strengthening K–12 Reporting Programs*, 2023.

Desai, Ishani, "Police Discuss How Campus Threats Are Investigated," *Bakersfield Californian*, June 1, 2022.

Dwyer, K., and D. Osher, "Safeguarding Our Children: An Action Guide," U.S. Departments of Education and Justice, American Institutes for Research, 2020.

ElSherief, Mai, Koustuv Saha, Pranshu Gupta, Shrija Mishra, Jordyn Seybolt, Jiajia Xie, Megan O'Toole, Sarah Burd-Sharps, and Munmun De Choudhury, "Impacts of School Shooter Drills on the Psychological Well-Being of American K–12 School Communities: A Social Media Study," *Humanities and Social Sciences Communications*, Vol. 8, No. 1, 2021.

FBI—*See* Federal Bureau of Investigation.

Federal Bureau of Investigation, "Think Before You Post: Hoax Threats Are Serious Federal Crimes," October 2018.

Federal Bureau of Investigation, "Multiple Agencies Warn of Posting Threats to Schools," FBI, El Paso, April 11, 2023.

Feldman, Eric, "The Consequences of Making Threats Against a School," WishTV.com, February 18, 2018.

Fleury, Isabelle, and Erin Dowdy, "Social Media Monitoring of Students for Harm and Threat Prevention: Ethical Considerations for School Psychologists," *Contemporary School Psychology*, Vol. 26, No. 3, 2022.

Grieco, Elizabeth, "For Many Rural Residents in the U.S., Local News Media Mostly Don't Cover the Area Where They Live," Pew Research Center, April 12, 2019.

Hankin, Abigail, Marci Hertz, and Thomas Simon, "Impacts of Metal Detector Use in Schools: Insights from 15 Years of Research," *Journal of School Health*, Vol. 81, No. 2, 2011.

Haskell, Josh, "FBI Says Threats Against Schools Increased 60 Percent Nationwide in 2022," ABC Eyewitness News, April 15, 2023.

Haskins, Caroline, "Gaggle Knows Everything About Teens and Kids in School," Buzzfeed News, November 1, 2019.

Hollywood, John S., Richard H. Donohue, Tara Richardson, Andrew Lauland, Cliff Karchmer, Jordan R. Reimer, Thomas Edward Goode, Dulani Woods, Pauline Moore, Patricia A. Stapleton, Erik E. Mueller, Mark Pope, and Tom Scott, *Mass Attacks Defense Toolkit*, RAND Corporation, TL-A1613-1, 2022. As of April 12, 2023:
https://www.rand.org/pubs/tools/TLA1613-1.html

Illinois Terrorism Task Force School Safety Working Group, "Communications Tips for School Threats," March 2018a.

Illinois Terrorism Task Force School Safety Working Group, "Response and Investigative Suggestions for School Threats," March 2018b.

I Love U Guys Foundation, *The Standard Response Protocol, K–12 Schools and Districts*, version 4.1, June 15, 2022.

Isger, Sonja, "School Threats: What Experts Say About How We Should Respond," Government Technology, February 17, 2016.

Jackson, Brian, Melissa Kay Diliberti, Pauline Moore, and Heather L. Schwartz, *Teachers' Views on School Safety: Consensus on Many Security Measures, but Stark Division About Arming Teachers*, RAND Corporation, RR-A2641-1, 2023. As of April 12, 2023: https://www.rand.org/pubs/research_reports/RRA2641-1.html

Jojola, Jeremy, and Steve Staeger, "Calls Reveal Swatter Threats That Caused Emergency Response to 17 Colorado Schools," 9News, February 23, 2023.

Keierleber, Mark, "Exclusive Data: An Inside Look at the Spy Tech That Followed Kids Home for Remote Learning—and Now Won't Leave," The 74 Million, September 24, 2021.

Kentucky Center for School Safety, "Elementary School Lockdown Workbook," undated.

Klein, Alyson, "TikTok Challenges Are a Nightmare for Schools: How Should Educators Respond?," *Education Week,* October 6, 2022.

Klinger, Amy, and Amanda Klinger, *Violent Threats and Incidents in Schools: An Analysis of the 2017–2018 School Year,* Educator's School Safety Network, 2018.

Koumpivola, Mila, "Chicago Public Schools Is Monitoring Students' Social Media for 'Worrisome Behavior,'" *Chalkbeat Chicago*, November 17, 2022.

Lankford, Adam, James Silver, and Jennifer Cox, "An Epidemiological Analysis of Public Mass Shooters and Active Shooters: Quantifying Key Differences Between Perpetrators and the General Population, Homicide Offenders, and People Who Die by Suicide," *Journal of Threat Assessment and Management*, Vol. 8, No. 4, 2021.

Lindberg, Nina, Atte Oksanen, Eila Sailas, and Riittakerttu Kaltiala-Heino, "Adolescents Expressing School Massacre Threats Online: Something to Be Extremely Worried About?," *Child and Adolescent Psychiatry and Mental Health*, Vol. 6, No. 1, 2012.

Lombardo, Clare, "After Parkland, Schools Grapple with Threats—and the Best Ways to Respond," NPR, April 14, 2018.

Mak, Aaron, "The Likely Truth About the 'National Shoot Up Your Schools Day' TikTok Trend," Slate, December 18, 2021.

Mascia, Jennifer, "How Lockdown Drills Can Retraumatize Kids Who Have Experienced Domestic Violence," The Trace, October 12, 2022.

Meloy, J. Reid, "Approaching and Attacking Public Figures: A Contemporary Analysis of Communications and Behavior," *Journal of Threat Assessment and Management*, Vol. 1, No. 4, 2014.

Meloy, J. Reid, J. Hoffmann, A. Guldimann, and D. James, "The Role of Warning Behaviors in Threat Assessment: An Exploration and Suggested Typology," *Behavioral Sciences & the Law*, Vol. 30, No. 3, 2012.

Middleton, Kyndra V., "The Longer-Term Impact of COVID-19 on K–12 Student Learning and Assessment," *Educational Measurement: Issues and Practice*, Vol. 39, No. 3, 2020.

Milkovich, M. C., "Managing Bomb Threats for School Administrators," American Academy of Experts in Traumatic Stress, 2020.

Mitchell, Melanie, and Gavan Palk, "Traversing the Space Between Threats and Violence: A Review of Threat Assessment Guidelines," *Psychiatry, Psychology and Law*, Vol. 23, No. 6, 2016.

Monagas, Enrique A., and Carlos E. Monagas, "Prosecuting Threats in the Age of Social Media," *Northern Illinois University Law Review*, Vol. 36, No. 3, 2015.

Moore, Pauline, Jennifer T. Leschitz, Brian A. Jackson, Catherine H. Augustine, Andrea Phillips, and Elizabeth D. Steiner, *Supporting Threat Reporting to Strengthen School Safety: Findings from the Literature and Interviews with Stakeholders Across the K–12 School Community*, RAND Corporation, RR-A1077-3, 2022. As of April 20, 2023: https://www.rand.org/pubs/research_reports/RRA1077-3.html

Moreschi, Angie, "School Violence Threats on Social Media Becoming Disruptive Trend," 11 News, February 18, 2022.

Mullen, Paul E., David V. James, J. Reid Meloy, Michele T. Pathé, Frank R. Farnham, Lulu Preston, Brian Darnley, and Jeremy Berman, "The Fixated and the Pursuit of Public Figures," *Journal of Forensic Psychiatry & Psychology*, Vol. 20, No. 1, 2009.

Natanson, Hannah, and Laura Meckler, "School Threats and Social Media Hoaxes Are Forcing Closures, Time-Consuming Investigations," *Washington Post*, December 20, 2021.

NASP and NASRO—*See* National Association of School Psychologists and National Association of School Resource Officers.

NASRO—*See* National Association of School Resource Officers.

National Association of School Psychologists and National Association of School Resource Officers, *Best Practice Considerations for Armed Assailant Drills in Schools*, April 2021.

National Association of School Resource Officers, "Surge in School 'Swatting' Calls: Considerations for School Resource Officers," September 26, 2022.

National Center for Campus Public Safety, *Guide to Social Media in Educational Environments*, 2016.

National Center for Education Statistics, "Table 214.40: Public Elementary and Secondary School Enrollment, Number of Schools, and Other Selected Characteristics, by Locale: Fall 2015 through Fall 2019," *Digest of Education Statistics*, undated.

National Emergency Number Association, "Public Safety Information on 'SWATTING,'" The 911 Association, undated.

National Police Foundation, *After-Action Review of the Orlando Fire Department Response to the Attack at Pulse Nightclub*, October 2018.

National Threat Assessment Center, *Enhancing School Safety Using a Threat Assessment Model: An Operational Guide for Preventing Targeted School Violence*, U.S. Secret Service, Department of Homeland Security, 2018.

National Threat Assessment Center, *Protecting America's Schools: A U.S. Secret Service Analysis of Targeted School Violence*, U.S. Department of Homeland Security, 2019.

National Threat Assessment Center, *Averting Targeted School Violence: A U.S. Secret Service Analysis of Plots Against Schools*, U.S. Department of Homeland Security, 2021.

NCES—*See* National Center for Education Statistics.

NENA—*See* National Emergency Number Association.

Newman, Andy, and Ali Watkins, "Hoax Shooting Threats Rattle New York Schools," *New York Times*, June 10, 2022.

Newman, Graeme, R., *Bomb Threats in Schools*, Problem-Oriented Guides for Police, Problem-Specific Guides Series, Guide No. 32, U.S. Department of Justice, August 2011.

Nieto-Munoz, Sophie, "HS Student Hurt After Jumping Through Window While 2 N.J. Schools Were on Lockdown," NJ.com, May 10, 2019.

NTAC—*See* National Threat Assessment Center.

O'Leary, Lizzie, "Why Expensive Social Media Monitoring Has Failed to Protect Schools," Slate, June 4, 2022.

Patton, Desmon Upton, Jun Sung Hong, Megan Ranney, Sadiq Patel, Caitlin Kelley, Rob Eschman, and Tyreasa Washington, "Social Media as a Vector for Youth Violence: A Review of the Literature," *Computers in Human Behavior*, Vol. 35, June 2014.

Perez, Angela Cordoba, "What Phoenix Policy, Districts Are Doing About Recent Threats in Schools," AZ Central, September 20, 2022.

Perumean-Chaney, Suzanne E., and Lindsay M. Sutton, "Students and Perceived School Safety: The Impact of School Security Measures," *American Journal of Criminal Justice*, Vol. 38, No. 4, 2013.

Peterson, Jillian, James Densley, David Riedman, Jamie Spaulding, and Hannah Malicky, "An Exploration of K–12 School Shooting Threats in the United States," *Journal of Threat Assessment and Management*, 2023.

Readiness and Emergency Management for Schools Technical Assistance Center, *Use of Social Media in School Behavioral Threat Assessments*, undated.

Regehr, Cheryl, Graham D. Glancy, Andrea Carter, and Lisa Ramshaw, "A Comprehensive Approach to Managing Threats of Violence on a University or College Campus," *International Journal of Law and Psychiatry*, Vol. 54, September–October 2017.

REMS TA Center—*See* Readiness and Emergency Management for Schools Technical Assistance.

Reynolds, Cristin Lee, R. Eric Platt, Lenore Malone Schaffer, and Holly Foster, "Social Media and Higher Education: The Problem of Anonymous Electronic Threats to the Campus Community," *Journal of Cases in Educational Leadership*, Vol. 20, No. 4, 2017.

Rich, Steven, and John Woodrow Cox, "'What If Someone Was Shooting?,'" *Washington Post*, December 26, 2018.

Riedman, David, K–12 School Shooting Database, 2023.

Safer Schools Together, "Basic Digital Threat Assessment Guide," undated-a.

Safer Schools Together, "Guidelines for Responding to Digital Threats," undated-b.

Safer Schools Together, Texas School Safety Center, and the International Center for Digital Threat Assessment, *Texas School Personnel's Guide to Social Media*, 2022.

Sanchez, Ray, Nicki Brown, and Brynn Gingras, "The 'Callous and Inhumane' School Shooting Hoaxes Are Still Happening Around the U.S.: Here's What We Know," CNN, November 19, 2022.

Santana, Steven, "Parents Clashed with San Antonio Officers During Jefferson High School Lockdown," mysanantonio.com, September 20, 2022.

Santucci, Jeanine, "Schools Across the U.S. Hit with Dozens of False Shooting, Bomb Threats: Experts Say It's a 'Cruel Hoax,'" *USA Today*, September 18, 2022.

Schildkraut, Jaclyn, and Amanda B. Nickerson, "Effects of Lockdown Drills on Students' Fear, Perceived Risk, and Use of Avoidance Behavior: A Quasi-Experimental Study," *Criminal Justice Policy Review*, Vol. 33, No. 8, 2022.

Schoeneman, Katherine. A., Mario. J. Scalora, C. D. Darrow, J. E. McLawsen, Grace. H. Chang, and William. J. Zimmerman, "Written Content Indicators of Problematic Approach Behavior Toward Political Officials," *Behavioral Sciences & the Law*, Vol. 29, No. 2, 2011.

Schoeneman-Morris, Katherine A., Mario J. Scalora, Grace H. Chang, William J. Zimmerman, and Yancey Garner, "A Comparison of Email Versus Letter Threat Contacts Toward Members of the United States Congress." *Journal of Forensic Sciences*, Vol. 52, No. 5, 2007.

School Safety Grant, "How Social Media Can Help Schools Deal with Threats," November 2020.

Schwartz, Reva, Apostol Vassilev, Kristen Greene, Lori Perine, Andrew Burt, and Patrick Hall, "Towards a Standard for Identifying and Managing Bias in Artificial Intelligence," NIST Special Publication 1270, March 2022.

Shade, Leslie Regan, and Rianka Singh, "'Honestly, We're Not Spying on Kids': School Surveillance of Young People's Social Media," *Social Media + Society*, Vol. 2, No. 4, 2016.

Shrestha, Amendra, Nazar Akrami, and Lisa Kaati, "Introducing Digital-7 Threat Assessment of Individuals in Digital Environments," IEEE/ACM International Conference on Advances in Social Networks Analysis and Mining (ASONAM), 2020.

Simons, André, and Ronald Tunkel, "The Assessment of Anonymous Threatening Communications," in J. Reid Melow and Jens Hoffman, eds., *International Handbook of Threat Assessment*, Oxford University Press, 2014.

Simpson, April, "As Local News Outlets Shutter, Rural America Suffers Most," Stateline, October 21, 2019.

Smith, Tim, "South Caroline School-Safety Bill Advances, Would Criminalize Threats Against Schools," *Greenville News*, March 13, 2018.

Stephenson, Cassandra, "Nashville Shooting Sheds Light on How to Handle Suicide Threats, What to Expect from Police," *The Tennessean*, March 31, 2023.

Straub, Frank, Blake Norton, Jennifer Zeunik, Brett Meade, Ben Gorban, Rebecca Benson, Joyce Iwashita, Charles Jennings, and Michael Johnson, *Regional Public Safety Communications in Broward County: A National Police Foundation Interim Review of the Impact of Communications Systems and Processes on Response to the February 14, 2018, Marjory Stoneman Douglas High School Shooting*, National Police Foundation, January 2019.

Stunson, Mike, "What Is the December 17 TikTok Challenge? Schools Across U.S. Cancel Classes, Up Security," *Charlotte Observer*, December 17, 2021.

Taylor, Derrick Bryson, Amanda Hopluch, and Maria Cramer, "Some U.S. Schools Close After Shooting Rumors," *New York Times*, December 17, 2021.

Trump, Kenneth, "Threat Assessment: School Threats, Social Media, Texting and Rumors," National School Safety and Security Services, undated.

Trump, Kenneth, "Study Finds Rapid Escalation of Violent School Threats," National School Safety and Security Services, 2016.

Tunkel, Ronald F., "Bomb Threat Assessments," *FBI Law Enforcement Bulletin*, Vol. 71, No. 10, 2002.

U.S. Department of Homeland Security, "Public Awareness Bulletin: Mitigating the Threat of School Violence as the U.S. 'Returns to Normal' from the COVID-19 Pandemic and Beyond," August 24, 2021.

U.S. Surgeon General's Office, *Social Media and Youth Mental Health: The U.S. Surgeon General's Advisory*, 2023.

Van Brunt, Brian, "Assessing Threat in Written Communications, Social Media, and Creative Writing," *Violence and Gender*, Vol. 3, No. 2, 2016.

Van Brunt, Brian, W. Scott Lewis, and Jeffrey H. Solomon, *The Challenge that Faces Us: An Educator's Guide to Assessing Threats in Student Writing*, Taylor and Francis Group, 2021.

Van der Vegt, Isabelle, Pippa Gregory, Bram B. van der Meer, Junyi Yang, Bennett Kleinberg, and Paul Gill, "Assessment Procedures in Anonymously Written Threats of Harm and Violence," *Journal of Threat Assessment and Management*, Vol. 9, No. 1, 2022.

Vo, Lam Thuy, and Peter Aldhous, "Your Dumb Tweets Are Getting Flagged to People Trying to Stop School Shootings," Buzzfeed News, October 31, 2019.

Vogels, Emily A., Rise Gelles-Watnick, and Navid Massarat, "Teens, Social Media and Technology 2022," Pew Research Center, August 10, 2022.

Wang, Ke, Jana Kemp, Riley Burr, and Deanne Swan, *Crime, Violence, Discipline, and Safety in U.S. Public Schools in 2019–2020: Findings from the School Survey on Crime and Safety*, NCES 2022-09, U.S. Department of Education, July 2022.

Ward, Micah, "How an Onslaught of Social Media Threats Is Disrupting and Terrorizing Schools," District Administration, May 9, 2023.

Williams, Kevin, Nicholas Bogel-Burroughs, and Tim Arango, "Gunman Who Killed Five in Louisville Left Note and Bought Rifle Legally," *New York Times*, April 11, 2023.

Winer, J. P., and R. P. Halgin, "Assessing and Responding to Threats of Targeted Violence by Adolescents: A Guide for Counselors," *Journal of Mental Health Counseling*, Vol. 38, No. 3, 2016.

Witsil, Frank, "School Threats Happening Daily Across Metro Detroit, Putting Students, Parents on Edge," *Detroit Free Press*, November 17, 2022.

Wong, Queenie, "Schools, Police Warn of U.S. School Shooting Threats on TikTok," CNET News, December 2021.

Wood, Sarah, "How Schools Are Handling TikTok Challenges," *U.S. News & World Report*, December 12, 2022.

Yechivi, Hannah, "Active Shooter Hoax Continues to Haunt Maine Schools," NewsCenterMaine.com, December 1, 2022.

Yousef, Odette, "False Calls About Active School Shooters Are Rising: Behind Them Is a Strange Pattern," NPR, October 7, 2022.